MODERN CHINA

Jonathan Clements

ALL THAT MATTERS

First published in Great Britain in 2013 by Hodder & Stoughton. An Hachette UK company.

First published in US in 2013 by The McGraw-Hill Companies, Inc.

British Library Cataloguing in Publication Data: a catalogue record for this title is available from the British Library.

Library of Congress Catalog Card Number: on file.

10 9 8 7 6 5 4 3 2 1

Typeset by Cenveo® Publisher Services.

Printed and bound in Great Britain by CPI Group (UK) Ltd., Croydon, CR0 4YY.

Hodder & Stoughton policy is to use papers that are natural, renewable and recyclable products and made from wood grown in sustainable forests. The logging and manufacturing processes are expected to conform to the environmental regulations of the country of origin.

Hodder & Stoughton Ltd

338 Euston Road

London NW1 3BH

www.hodder.co.uk

Also available in ebook

About the author

Jonathan Clements studied Mandarin at National Cheng Chi University, Taiwan. He is the author of many publications about China, including a history of Beijing and biographies of Chairman Mao, Empress Wu and the diplomat Wellington Koo. The Chinese translation of his book on the First Emperor was published in the People's Republic in 2007. He was a consultant and interviewee on the National Geographic documentary *Koxinga: A Hero's Legacy*, which drew heavily on his book *Pirate King*. His most recent work is *The Art of War: A New Translation*, which revisits Sun Tzu's military classic in the modern age.

He wrote the 'Asia & the World' chapters for the Oxford University Press *Big Ideas* history series, which won an Australian Publishing Association award for Excellence in Educational Publishing. In 2011, he was appointed as a Contributing Editor to the online *Encyclopedia of Science Fiction*, with special responsibility for China and Japan. His 50+ China entries form a book-within-a-book, charting the genre's use as a tool for Party propaganda, state-approved technocracy and subtle dissidence.

Contents

Introduction:
the matter of China

*Since China was still unknown,
every kind of nonsense was
conveyed to us about that country.
That imbecilic and barbarous
government, which a handful of
Europeans manipulated at will,
seemed... the most complete
model that all the nations of the
world might copy.*

*Alexis de Tocqueville, Ancien Regime and
the French Revolution (1856)*

The question of 'all that matters' depends on whom it matters *to*. Historically, that means understanding the issues that were important to the decision-makers and participants in past events. Politically, it also means considering the implications of events – why they happen, and what they mean for both the Chinese and ourselves. But it also means considering those issues in modern China that will matter in the future. This book, short as it is, aims to equip the reader with the names, dates and issues liable to crop up in conversation among modern China-watchers.

Inevitably, there are immense differences of opinion. Tang Xiaoju's cogent, 146-page *Concise History of the Communist Party of China* consigns the years 1957–78, spanning the Great Leap Forward and the Cultural Revolution, to a single page, conceding only that it was a period that contained 'long-term mistakes'. There are surely hardliners and cadres who would say that the period genuinely doesn't matter *to the Party*. But it certainly matters to the millions who died.

To polite society in Victorian England, it only mattered that tea came from China, not that British traders often bartered it for cripplingly addictive opium. To threatened village headmen in rural China, it mattered that strange foreign preachers and merchants were upsetting the traditional order, not that they brought prospects of education, hygiene and development. To the foreign traders and their families who huddled, terrified, in Beijing's Legation Quarter during the Boxer Rebellion, it mattered that a millennial cult of martial artists wanted to murder them, not that the mobs themselves were often operating with the secret support of the ruling regime. Modern students from the People's Republic of China (PRC) know all about the Opium Wars and the Century of Humiliation, but are often under-informed about the worst excesses of the Mao era; what matters to them is often a world away, in an online game or an iPhone app. They, in turn, may not realize what is kept from them – from gaming consoles shut out of the Chinese market, to anything controversial on the internet, filtered out of sight by the government's 'Golden Shield' censorship squad.

For the foreign reader, Chinese history can be a distracting whirl of monosyllabic names and forgotten dynasties. This book homes in on the most crucial factors influencing modern Chinese life and culture, concentrating in particular on the legacies of two very different men, Mao Zedong and Deng Xiaoping, and the potential of a new generation, currently represented (but not necessarily embodied) by the incumbent President Xi Jinping.

Chapter 1 marks the beginning of 'Modern China' in the triumphant declaration of the People's Republic, and the troubled three decades that followed. A self-proclaimed Marxist utopia, China struggled with its early love affair with Soviet Russia, and soon drifted off-message. The Cold War era found China shut off from much international contact, instead gnawing on itself in a series of disastrous social experiments. While Communist propaganda proclaimed unanimity of purpose and belief, the Party was torn apart in internal conflicts and vendettas, fought with falsified statistics and military patronage. Realistic five-year economic plans were transformed into grotesque, fantastical Great Leaps and inner revolutions.

Chapter 2 marks the last and most enduring change in direction, as the new order of Deng Xiaoping subtly spurned Mao and embraced 'socialism with Chinese characteristics'. Deng's economic reforms, often implemented by proxies who took the heat for any setbacks, created an overwhelming, world-changing period of rapid growth. One-horse towns ballooned into glittering cities, and China became a powerhouse of exports and investment. This, of course, brought a whole new series of issues to light – particularly social injustice and inequalities of opportunity. To paraphrase the writer William Gibson, the future had arrived, but it was not evenly distributed. Deng deliberately avoided a personality cult like that of Mao, but his influence on modern China is arguably even greater than that of the Chairman whose face still scowls out from Chinese banknotes. In terms of the meteoric rise and boggling successes of contemporary China, Deng matters a great deal more.

Chapter 3 tells the story of China's approaches to its own periphery, in particular the 1997 handover of Hong Kong, one of the pivotal events of modern times. Through Hong Kong, we can examine the story of China's recovery from the humiliations of the Victorian era, but also the likely development of Chinese policy towards the issues of Taiwan and Tibet. The leader of China during this period was the stony-faced Jiang Zemin, although much of the achievement remained a continuation of Deng's legacy.

Chapter 4 charts the first decade of the 21st century, symbolised by the Beijing Olympics. However, the iconic sight of Communist China hosting the world's greatest sporting event did not come without its controversies. The chapter goes on to ask who the Chinese really are – pundits talk of a billion consumers, as if China presents the same single, homogeneous face that it presented to the world in the Mao era, but there are many subgroups within the catch-all title of 'the Chinese', many of them with populations that dwarf entire foreign countries. The Communist Party alone has 82 million members, making it an entity with a larger population than Germany. But there are also more Muslims in China than Swedes in Sweden. What of the urban and rural Chinese? The rich and poor...?

Chapter 5 weighs the likely problems as China grapples with the same large-scale issues that beset Western capitalism. China's participation in a global market has confronted it with transnational issues in ecology, sustainability and trade, but also highlighted the influence that China exerts on the rest of the world. Two centuries after an isolationist China was carved up by foreign powers, China itself faces the prospect of a new form of empire, involving itself intimately in many overseas economies. When contaminants in the Chinese food chain are exported to American supermarkets, when Chinese hydroelectric schemes dry up rivers in neighbouring South-East Asian countries, when Chinese banks become the main investors in entire sectors of international business, China matters deeply, even for those who have never considered it. This final chapter takes as its template the Twelfth Five-Year Plan, which collates the Chinese government's own think-tank advice on what will matter to it in the year 2015 and beyond.

It is difficult, impossible in fact, to contain the multitudes of a nation more than a billion strong, across seventy years of modern history, within a book of this size. We can only delineate the major players in the broadest possible strokes; inevitably there will be omissions. There is little space here for the squabbles, putsches and ideological spats that characterize Chinese politics. The volatile nature of Communist Party discourse favours the anonymous over the flamboyant, and the charmless over the charismatic; this, in turn, makes many speeches and proclamations unbearably tedious. Accordingly, I have made quotes as brief and pithy as possible. As the narrative drifts towards the present day, I have favoured the reportage that is most memorable and iconic. At times, this may seem as if I am trivializing important issues in favour of gossip and internet memes, but this is all part of an attempt to create an impression of all that matters, at this moment.

The 100 Ideas section, common to the *All That Matters* series, is used here to point the reader at larger books and online resources that can afford to concentrate in depth on the issues over which I must necessarily skate.

▶ The Century of Humiliation

Chinese school textbooks refer to a 'Century of Humiliation' stretching from roughly 1839 to 1949, in which China was set upon, colonized and exploited by agents of foreign powers. Gunboat diplomacy forced open Chinese ports to trade, and the Opium Wars defended the decision of the British to sell drugs. The island of Hong Kong was ceded to the British in 1841, but was only one of dozens of areas that were carved up between foreign powers. As just a few examples,

Russia seized a million square kilometres of territory on the Pacific coast in 1858, the British and Russians were all too swift to recognize a breakaway Muslim republic that flourished in the hinterland in the 1870s (the state of Kashgaria, which fell apart after the death of its primary leader in 1877), the French occupied Indochina in the 1880s, the Japanese seized Korea and Taiwan in the 1890s, the British briefly invaded Tibet in the 1900s, Russia supported an independent Mongolia in 1921 and Japan occupied Manchuria in the 1930s.

China began the 20th century as a failing state. The centuries-old Qing dynasty, dominated for decades by the conservative Empress Dowager, was powerless to resist such incursions by modern Europeans, who had carved out treaty ports for themselves at harbours, river ports and inland rail-heads in what came to be known as the Unequal Treaties. Resistance took a variety of forms, most infamously in the Boxer Rebellion, in which disaffected peasants took up arms against foreign traders and missionaries.

Some traditionally-minded Chinese saw a problem not with the system itself, but with its administrators, and agitated for the overthrow of the Qing dynasty, which was descended from Manchu invaders, and its replacement with a new, ethnically Chinese dynasty. That, at least, was the claim – in some cases, such 'reformers' were simply warlords and bandit leaders. Others, including some within the Qing dynasty itself, hoped for a constitutional monarchy that would keep the Emperor in power. Still others wanted the removal of the imperial system in its entirety, and its replacement with a republic.

The Last Emperor, 'Henry' Puyi (1906–67) was overthrown in the revolution of 1911, and the Republic of China was proclaimed on 1 January 1912. However, there was no easy transition. A second revolution broke out in 1913, effectively bisecting China into north and south. The republican Chinese were mired in violent factionalism, and the warlord who had secured the Emperor's abdication fleetingly declared himself to be a new emperor in 1915. The fighting would go on, in one form or another, for decades.

▶ The May Fourth Movement

When 140,000 Chinese men went to Europe to take part in the Great War of 1914–18, they moved an amount of earth equivalent to a new Great Wall, but underground, digging many of the infamous trenches of France. They fetched and carried, laundered and cooked, and worked in factories to replace the many European men sent to the frontline. Hundreds of them are commemorated in French cemeteries, victims of stray bombs and equal-opportunity influenza, but they are largely forgotten in the story of the Great War, at least as far as it matters to the Allies. The Chinese were literally painted over in the Parisian *Panthéon de la Guerre* monument, in order to make room for the arrival of the Americans.

China's entry into WW1 was an attempt to be taken seriously as a modern nation, and to secure the return of the province of Shandong, which had been in German hands since 1897. Instead, Chinese delegates at the

Paris Peace Conference of 1919 were left aghast as the coalition of Great Powers awarded Shandong to the Japanese, effectively reassigning occupied Chinese territory to a new colonial master. The decision was a turning point in Chinese history, alienating many of the reformers who had previously supported co-operation with the Western powers. Unable to look either back to the imperial era or forward to further humiliations at the hands of the international community, many in China chose to step sideways, towards the bright red promises of the newly formed Soviet Union.

The May Fourth Movement of cultural and political protests, also known as the New Culture Movement, was a grass-roots effort to cast aside the mistakes of the past and embrace ideas that would strengthen China, sometimes welcomed as the symbolic figures 'Mr Science' and 'Mr Democracy'. This took many forms, including modernist, realist literature and debates on democracy and women's liberation, but above all a movement that doubted Chinese tradition. Patriarchy, imperial rule and the assumption that China was the centre of the world were all outmoded concepts. Instead of continually hearkening back to mythical pasts and legendary paragons, the youthful thinkers of the May Fourth Movement demanded that China look to the future.

Chinese politics turned into an uneasy, threatening standoff between Nationalists (the Kuomintang) and Communists, a civil war that lasted from 1927 to 1950. This, however, was obscured by a third front, as the invading Japanese in the 1930s met with a Chinese resistance that was occasionally united against them. With the defeat of the Japanese in 1945, the two Chinese factions turned once more upon each other, until the Communists prevailed.

▶ Past matters

The narrative of the Century of Humiliation has left the Chinese, particularly those who are products of its contemporary education system, hypersensitive to matters of 'the sovereignty and integrity of territory'. Anything that seems to be an incursion on Chinese soil, from the bombing of an embassy in the former Yugoslavia, to Japanese fishing boats off the Senkaku Islands, to attempts by the US Securities and Exchange Commission to audit the books of Chinese companies, can open old wounds.

The Communist Party did not exist at the time of the Unequal Treaties, and hence is able to spin the history of the Century of Humiliation as a story with two bad guys – the outmoded Qing dynasty and the evil foreign imperialists. Unfortunately, this can leave the People's Republic blissfully unaware of those times when its own behaviour resembles those of its old-time bugbears.

Meanwhile, the May Fourth Movement contained within it the seeds of much of China's subsequent development in the 20th century. It was a touchstone for both Mao Zedong and Deng Xiaoping in the implementation of their own reforms, and its echoes continue to resound today. One might argue that the People's Republic has fulfilled many of the aims of the May Fourth Movement apart from democracy; a can of worms that cannot be opened, for a Communist state should, by definition, already represent the ultimate expression of the will of its people.

1

The East is red

Communism is not love. Communism is a hammer which we use to crush the enemy.

Mao Zedong

On 1 October 1949, Chairman Mao Zedong climbed the steps to the gallery of the Gate of Heavenly Peace (*Tiananmen*), the elaborate bastion that sits at the southern entrance to the Forbidden City in Beijing. There, among the assembled dignitaries of his Party, he addressed a crowd in the open space in front of the gate with the famous words: 'We, the 475 million Chinese people, have stood up, and our future is infinitely bright.'

Reporting of the event is often compromised by anachronisms. Not the least is the belief that Mao was the 'leader' of China – although he was the Chairman of the Party, the official head of state was Zhou Enlai (1898–1976). Many authors claim that he addressed a crowd of 100,000 in Tiananmen Square, although the design and implementation of that famous assembly ground had yet to be undertaken. Moreover, he was merely summarizing an earlier speech, given to a smaller crowd of 600, ten days earlier at a conference to ratify an interim constitution.

Mao's speech to the Political Consultative Conference, 21 September 1949

[T]he Chinese people, comprising one quarter of humanity, have now stood up. The Chinese have always been a great, courageous and industrious nation; it is only in modern times that they have fallen behind. And that was due entirely to oppression and exploitation by foreign imperialism and domestic reactionary governments. For over a century our forefathers never stopped waging unyielding struggles against domestic and foreign oppressors, including the Revolution

▲ Chairman Mao.

of 1911 led by Dr Sun Yat-sen, our great forerunner in the Chinese revolution. ... From now on our nation will belong to the community of the peace-loving and freedom-loving nations of the world and work courageously and industriously to foster its own civilization and well-being and at the same time to promote world peace and freedom. Ours will no longer be a nation subject to insult and humiliation.

The Gate of Heavenly Peace was traditionally the location from which the Emperors' proclamations had been decreed. Even amid the buzzwords of revolution and radical change, there was the implication that it would be business as usual. But Mao's imperial airs were nothing new. As early as 1944, he had been depicted planting the first grains of millet at sowing time – formerly the duty of the Emperor. Songs proclaimed his glory, and propaganda pictures did not shy from presenting him surrounded by a deifying sunburst.

Mao's true heyday was the 1940s, when he had somehow survived the intrigues of the Communist Party at bay to be regarded as its political driving force. But while Mao was an inspiring, charismatic leader in war, he could be catastrophically inept in peacetime. The personality cult that grew up around him – whose effects can still be felt today in tacky Mao memorabilia, his Tiananmen mausoleum and a handful of surviving statues – was something of an afterthought. It was a fire fanned by both his friends and his foes, seeking to reassert his role in the state, but also to distract him and his supporters while others manoeuvred for true power.

Even as Mao bragged that 'the Chinese people have stood up', the Nationalists were still fighting in defence of Chongqing. Much of southwest China was still in Nationalist hands, and a failed attempt to take the coastal island of Quemoy had cost 9,000 casualties. The Nationalists were eventually routed from the mainland, moving to the island enclave of Taiwan, where their leader, Chiang Kai-shek, would remain a constant reminder of the Other China.

▲ A propaganda poster from circa 1960, proclaiming: 'May the Whole Country from the Mountains to the Rivers be a Sea of Red'.

Taiwan has been an anomaly ever since – a redoubt of the Nationalist 'Republic of China' that continued to occupy the Chinese seat on the UN Security Council until 1971. This, in turn, implied a readiness on the part of the Western world to believe that Communist China was a passing fad, and that the US-backed, non-Communist Taiwan would eventually return to reclaim the Mainland. Meanwhile, Communist China began the 1950s with every intention of reclaiming Taiwan in an amphibious assault. Although it would periodically allude to this in the years to come, the outbreak of the Korean War forced China to move many troops away from the southwest coast to the north. By the mid-1950s, China had other priorities, and the Nationalists remained entrenched in their new home. Taiwan itself did not lift martial law until 1987.

By the beginning of the 1950s, we might consider the mindset of the generation among the Communists that had overthrown the Emperor, spent 15 years fighting the Japanese and four further years in civil war, and after only the briefest respite was plunged straight into a war in Korea. It mattered very much to the PRC that it seemed to be beset on all sides: by the Soviet Union (soon no longer a friend), by US interference in Southeast Asia, and by the US-supported regimes in South Korea, Japan and Taiwan.

▶ The first Five-Year Plan

With rice-growing areas far from coal-mining areas, far in turn from forests, far in turn from wheat fields, there is a certain rationale to be found in Chinese centralized control. In particular, land use in China often relies on rigorous regulation of water, in terms of both crop irrigation and flood prevention, which in turn favours large-scale enterprises to maintain levees and water courses. After the ceasefire in Korea, China turned to a Soviet-influenced model for national renewal and reform – a series of targets and policies known as the First Five-Year Plan. Soviet 'advisers' arrived in China to build 156 factories among a total of 694 construction projects, while across the rest of the country, business owners were 'encouraged' to sell or hand over their enterprises to state control. The aim, largely successful, was to remove all private ownership; by the end of the period more than half of China's businesses were state-owned, and the rest were public–private partnerships. Handicraft industries were reorganized into co-operatives. Farmers were encouraged to merge their lands into ever-larger co-operatives with their neighbours. At first, one's wealth had a factor in the rewards, as income was based on the amount of *land* that each farmer brought to the collective. However, later stages of the organization rearranged income to be generated solely from *labour*, so that each individual only received returns equal to the physical work they put in. Many families retained a small plot of land for their own private use, but it was specifically for subsistence.

▶ Simplified Chinese

One of the achievements of the period was a simplification and rationalization of the Chinese language. For the Chinese themselves, this took the form of an overhaul of the writing system, in which many complex symbols were replaced by significantly simpler ones. In many cases, these versions had already been in use, sometimes for centuries, as abbreviations – now Mao proclaimed that they were the new orthodoxy. As part of the simplification process, many homophones were now represented by the same character instead of more complex versions. The reform of the writing system was intended to aid literacy among China's people, and while it certainly made the language easier to learn in schools, it also created a generation of young Chinese who would struggle to read many documents written before 1952. Henceforth, Mainland Chinese would require additional schooling to accurately read any materials written for the overseas Chinese market in territories such as Hong Kong or Taiwan, making the Party line not only official, but also often unchallenged. The reform also eliminated many shades of meaning and poetic variants – while not quite an Orwellian Newspeak, it certainly helped establish the founding of the People's Republic as a Year Zero.

A similar reform, more apparent to foreigners, altered the way that Chinese was spelled with Roman letters. Previous attempts to spell Chinese been concocted by missionaries and academics, often allowing localized accents to creep into their decisions, or haphazardly attempted by the Chinese themselves. Now, the PRC decided how to 'Romanize' Chinese, selecting official spellings that were largely much closer to the way Chinese actually sounded. Peking, for example, a word that always carried within it a whisper of a Cantonese accent, was now Beijing. Mao Tse-tung was now Mao

Zedong. As with the internal reform of Chinese characters, this supposed simplification of spelling often created two or more versions of the same place name, used by different generations. Some places, like Shanghai or Chengdu, were fortunate to remain unchanged. Others, like Nanking, suffered a consonantal change (to Nanjing) that can still confuse foreigners today.

▶ The 'five daggers' and the 'hundred flowers'

Government interference in the writing system was accompanied by invasive new controls over public thought. As with many policies implemented when the Communist Party came to power, it involved a reversal of promises made during the revolutionary struggle. Mao's 'On New Democracy' (1940) had called for censure of imperialists and Nationalists, but had otherwise supported intellectual freedom. Now in power, and with an authority that rested largely on his interpretation of Communist ideology, Mao pulled the rug out from under other Party members. The author Liang Shuming had often discussed the contradictions between traditional, Confucian Chinese society, Western individualism and Marxist class struggle. Now, Mao attacked Liang for even suggesting that there was any alternative to the last. What started as a debate swiftly turned into public criticism, and Liang was hounded for the rest of his career.

In 1954, the writer Hu Feng, a leading light of the May Fourth Movement and a Party member, wrote a long report concerning the 'five daggers' now pointed at Chinese creativity: strict adherence to a Marxist worldview; an emphasis on reforming thought; the insistence on covering only issues affecting peasants, soldiers and the working class, a refusal to consider new literary paradigms; and a drift towards 'sunny subjects' in order to avoid any accusations of cynicism. It was submitted directly to the Party's Central Committee, seemingly in the belief that there was still hope of reform. Although Hu's protest was a remarkable prediction of the Orwellian future for Chinese literature in the next few decades, many of Hu's fellow authors joined in public attacks on him, at Mao's urging, for daring to speak what many of them were thinking. Arrested as a counter-revolutionary along with hundreds of sympathizers, he would languish in prison until 1979.

▲ As Maoism took hold, even the arts were expected to function as part of the rhetoric of Communism.

Having made it clear that he was judge and jury of how cultural policy should proceed, Mao also seized with nit-picking pedantry on other targets. A 1956 film, about a 19th-century orphan who ran a charity for rural educational reforms, met with mild praise from Party grandees. Mao, however, wrote a stinging and initially anonymous review in the People's Daily, pointing out that the hero was little more than a stooge of the establishment, going cap-in-hand to landlords and nobles and *begging* for aid that the people deserved by right.

By 1957, facing reversals of certain dogma from the Soviet bloc, as well as problems within the first Five-Year Plan, Mao changed his tune, suggesting in his speech 'On the Correct Handling of Contradictions among the People' that some criticism and protest was helpful. Not for the last time, his words hid a conflict within the Party that he hoped to supress by enlisting the people themselves, calling for criticism with the famous phrase: 'Let a hundred flowers boom; let a hundred schools of thought contend.' His rival Liu Shaoqi meekly suggested that flowers required a 'gentle breeze and fine rain', although Mao's words were soon taken up in strikes, beatings and purges within the Party.

After a brief flurry of open criticism, many who spoke their mind were dismissed from their posts, demoted, exiled or imprisoned. Mao bragged to his colleagues that it had been his plan all along: 'How can we catch the snakes if we don't let them out of their lairs? We wanted those [bastards] to wriggle and sing and fart... that way we can catch them.' However, it seems more likely that he had originally expected his ideology to stand up to criticism and debate, and had turned on his critics when they dared to find flaws.

The deals between China and Soviet Russia had largely worked out in Russia's favour. Although Nikita Khrushchev visited China amid great fanfare in order to hand back the Russian treaty port of Lushun, great swathes of formerly Chinese territory remained uncontested in Russian hands, including Outer Mongolia – once part of Qing China, now a Russian satellite state – and much of the Russian Far East, which had been snatched from China in 1858. In 1956 Khrushchev made a speech criticizing Stalin and his personality cult. This implied not only that a Communist state could make mistakes, but also that the Chinese had done so by following the Russian line. Mao began to grumble that the Soviets were losing sight of their ideals, and were even drifting once more towards capitalism. Lifting an already contentious term from the works of Marx and Trotsky, Mao spoke of a 'permanent revolution', in which the people of China would have to consistently and continuously struggle to keep capitalism from re-asserting itself.

Mao's 'On the Correct Handling of Contradictions among the People', 27 February 1957

Marxists are still a minority among the entire population as well as among the intellectuals. Therefore, Marxism must still develop through struggle. Marxism can develop only through struggle, and not only is this true of the past and the present, it is necessarily true of the future as well. What is correct invariably develops in the course of struggle with what is wrong. ... Such struggles will never end.

Karl Marx had argued that revolution would find its origins in disaffected urban workers, but China's urban workforce was relatively tiny. 'Maoism', as Mao Zedong Thought has come to be known, was instead a shaky application of fragments of Marxism to a peasant-based economy. Mao could not read any foreign languages, and seemed to have a tenuous, second-hand grasp of many Marxist ideas – he never referred, for example, to the 'Asian Mode of Production', which would surely have been top of his list for comments if he had heard of it. Mao had been one of the last students to be trained in the centuries-old Confucian education system, abolished in 1905, which favoured poetry and essays on the ancient classics. It was all but useless in an economy that required engineers and scientists, and left him perpetually on the defensive, belittling his critics with pithy one-liners that often alluded to old folktales, or implied that he had some sort of mystic 'political' insight that had eluded them.

▶ The Great Leap Forward

The approach of the tenth anniversary of the founding of the People's Republic saw several large-scale architectural projects designed to celebrate and commemorate the historic event. It was at this time that Tiananmen 'Square' acquired much of its contemporary appearance. A centrepiece, the Gate of China, had been demolished in 1954. Now the open space was significantly widened, and its edges became the sites of the Great Hall of the People and the Museum of Revolutionary History. The aim was specifically to construct a parade ground to rival Red Square in Moscow.

Big buildings in Beijing went together with even grander schemes in China as a whole. The most infamous was Mao's 'Great Leap Forward', in which the Chairman determined to increase China's productivity in one massive, concerted national effort. Writing off many Party advisers as 'zombies with a slave mentality', Mao demanded that the country's new direction should be 'blazing red', enough to surpass the British economy within 15 years. This called for massive agricultural increases, which themselves required massive irrigation programmes – at the grassroots level, this inevitably meant conscripting thousands of peasants into work gangs to dig new trenches and canals. Steel was the building block of all other industries, leading officials all over China to promise ever more unrealistic quotas, to meet equally unlikely demands for road- and factory-building programmes from their counterparts. Such grade inflation occurred at every level of the administration, until a relatively realistic goal at the managerial end had been bumped up by over-eager promises and one-upmanship into demands at the local level for up to six times existing levels of productivity.

Meeting such demands required drastic measures. Some areas set up large-scale communes, in which all private land was abolished, and workers were forced to live together under military conditions in order to maximize their productivity. Those who attempted to lessen expectations, or cautioned against such measures, were cast out for their negativity or 'superstition', whereas the only superstition in evidence was blind faith in Mao's vision. With no scientific or engineering background, Mao offered the blandest and least helpful of managerial exhortations – that simply believing in his targets would be enough to get things done. The plan combined fanatical faith in a dictator, a crass disregard for the evidence and an embittered, post-colonial belief that China's failings were merely a state of mind engendered by foreign oppression. Freed from imperialist exploitation and misguided Soviet advice, Mao's China would surely now leap into the future, with a quantum increase in productivity that Mao openly likened to an 'explosion' of pent-up energy.

To make matters worse, August 1958 brought a fantastic harvest, as if the elements themselves were bending to Mao's will. Buoyed up with enthusiasm, he doubled the previous year's steel targets. China gained 25,000 communes, each of them equivalent to a small town, eating in large mess halls and casting aside money in favour of points earned for labours done. Presented with iron that was falsely claimed to have been smelted in a backyard furnace, Mao endorsed the setting-up of thousands of similar cottage enterprises, reaching for his steel quotas by melting down 'scrap metal' such as the pots and pans no longer required in private kitchens.

The Great Leap Forward of 1958–61 offered a series of parables of the dangers of interfering with delicate systems – with cascade effects that only served to worsen conditions. In one of the most infamous exercises in social engineering, Mao decided that sparrows were an unwelcome burden on the nation's grain production. Peasants were encouraged to catch and kill the pests, and a nationwide campaign ran around the clock to exhaust the birds by refusing to allow them to land or rest until they dropped from the sky. In successfully wiping out sparrows, the Chinese also removed the main predator that kept down numerous varieties of insects, leading to epidemics of bed bugs and grain-eating locusts.

Meanwhile, the mass smelting operations generated millions of tonnes of useless, low-grade iron, while eating up vast quantities of much-needed coal. In the scramble for fuel, coal was replaced with wood, not only inefficient for furnaces, but also denuding hillsides of the trees that held back landslides. Commune kitchen managers, believing that they were living in a time of plenty, burned through several months' food supply in days and did not dare report that they were running low. Outlying provinces attempted to save face by wildly over-reporting their successes, with propaganda now used not to encourage further efforts, but to claim that current efforts were already succeeding. The author Chi Shuchang speculated about the prospects of breeding pigs the size of elephants in order to match the artistic licence of one famous propaganda image. With Orwellian zeal, the press claimed that the corn in some Chinese fields grew so thick and close together that rats could not enter the fields, and children could walk atop the stalks. Less widely reported was the truth, that while the 1958 harvest was bountiful, there were not enough workers to bring in the crops, as too many had been reassigned to the wild-goose chase of iron smelting. Precious wheat was left to rot in the fields, and Mao would later confess in a closed meeting that it had not occurred to him that not only iron and steel, but also wheat, required a transport system to move it around.

Belatedly realizing that he was looking at falsified figures, Mao revised the following year's targets, dropping them by 30 per cent, seemingly unaware they were still 30 per cent higher than the current year's actual results. China entered 1959 with targets that were still impossible, but the fat years, such as they were, were over. 1959 brought droughts, famine and a revolt in Tibet that saw the Dalai Lama run for India. Mao resigned as Party chairman, putting on a show of self-criticism, but actually leaving his successor to carry the can for the failed Great Leap policies. In the years that followed, the vicious circle of policies led to millions of further deaths, the situation aggravated still further by a decision to leave some lands fallow in order to avoid a surplus of non-existent, phantom grain, and by the continued export of grain to pay debts to the Soviets. Unhelpfully, the Yellow River burst its banks, causing more deaths from flooding and destroying more crops. A conservative estimate places the total number of deaths from starvation and unrest at 30 million. Mao's Great Leap ended with stories of murder and cannibalism.

▶ The Cultural Revolution

Paranoia had set in. China tested its first nuclear device in 1964, amid Cold War concerns that the Soviet Union might unleash a first strike at any moment. A warren of tunnels still exists beneath the streets of Beijing, dug by hand by thousands of labourers preparing to wait out an atomic attack. Mao fretted that the Chinese were complacent after the Great Leap, and were tempted by 'economism' – which is to say that they were satisfied with the new status quo, forgetting that the revolution was not yet over. The generation born after 1945 had grown up without any direct experience of war, and did not, in Mao's view, appreciate the struggles of their elders. Perhaps more importantly for Mao, these same children had grown up knowing nothing but the personality cult of Chairman Mao. These 'Red Guards' were a force that he could use against his contemporaries, united by their faith in his *Quotations*, a.k.a. 'the Little Red Book'.

It was a deadly cocktail. Mao's urgings for a revolution of the heart set angry, resentful, passionate teenagers with guns and a sense of entitlement against anything that might be defined as anti-Communist. The result was thuggish and wilfully ignorant, attacking teachers for their sense of superiority, engineers for their hoarding of knowledge, and doctors for their claims to know something about the health of others. The quest for equality turned into a witch hunt against anyone who had bettered themselves, and a racist, hate-filled campaign against anyone who seemed 'different',

炮打司令部
（我的一张大字报）

无产阶级文化大革命全面胜利万岁

▲ Propaganda poster reading 'May the Great Proletarian Cultural Revolution Thrive for 10,000 Years'.

including ethnic minorities, the religious and those who were associated in any way with foreigners or foreign ideas. Mosques and temples were burned, statues of Confucius and other intellectual figures were smashed, and the looting, rioting youth were eventually reined in only by the intervention of the People's Liberation Army.

The worst was over by the end of the 1960s, but it would take another decade to undo the damage. China entered the 1970s as a terrifying Communist self-parody, with a population so afraid of difference that everybody even dressed the same. Mao's proclaimed aim for the Cultural Revolution was to fight against 'those in authority pursuing the capitalist road'. It effectively pitted the children of the revolution against certain sectors of the founding fathers, setting teenagers who had grown up with nothing but Communist Party rhetoric against those among their elders who might still retain elements of the capitalist tradition. Below the surface, it amounted to a purge of anyone who had dared to blame Mao for the disasters of the Great Leap Forward, accusing them of lacking sufficient understanding of what was required to create a Communist utopia. Such luckless individuals were not to be 'punished', but 're-educated' – packed off to remote farms to learn what life was like for the peasants. As with the purges of the revolution itself, the definition of these 'capitalist roaders' was soon expanded to include anyone embodying any potential friction for Communist ideals, which soon led to the removal of people with families in unapproved professions, with educational qualifications that might have given them airs, with capitalist relatives abroad or with ethnic identities (such as Tibetans or Manchus) that might lead others to question their loyalty to the Communist cause.

▶ Mao matters

Mao is the dead, red heart of modern China. His corpse lies in its mausoleum in Beijing's Tiananmen Square, in full view of the centre of government, and his portrait still adorns the front of the Gate of Heavenly Peace. His image can still be seen on Chinese banknotes, and even on illegal 'ghost money' burned by the superstitious to appease evil spirits. He has, in effect, attained divine status, bolstered not only by the memories of the old, but also by the ignorance of the young.

▲ Illegal for being both counterfeit and superstitious, this 10 million Yuan Bank of Hell note is 'ghost money' for burning in offering to one's ancestors.

Mao Zedong Thought has been radically redacted for posterity. Even while Mao was still alive, the official canon favoured his early works and speeches from the war era, and swiftly petered out after the founding of the Republic in 1949. Barely 10 per cent of the *Selected Readings* come from after 1957, when his train of thought might reasonably be said to have gone right off the rails. The infamous Little Red Book, compiled in 1964 and eventually printed in over a billion copies in over 40 languages, was similarly biased towards his early days. The official Party line, as parsed by Deng Xiaoping in the 1980s, is that Mao was a great statesman who 'made mistakes', although the genocidal magnitude of those mistakes, and the terrifying human cost, is rarely discussed. It is not uncommon to hear the Chinese parrot Deng Xiaoping's comment that Mao was '70 per cent good and 30 per cent bad', as if the existence of a cod-statistical ruling on the matter has effectively closed the discussion.

Mao is a powerful symbol. For a Communist Party that has dismantled so many of his policies and ideas, his image remains as a unifying symbol that all can agree upon – the last tenuous tie that keeps the Party from being nothing more than an elite of self-interested oligarchs and technocrats. Mao was the great architect of modern China, to whom all must genuflect, even if the policies they enact in his name are the polar opposite of what he did himself. The question of what Mao would have done given any new circumstances is implicit in every debate and reformist programme in China, a presumption of theoretical immortality, as if Mao were somehow magically still alive, 120-plus years old, and adapting to the times.

The teenagers who smashed up temples and tortured their teachers in the Cultural Revolution are now in their 60s and 70s. They are the generation currently running China, the politicians and bureaucrats glad-handing each other at banquets and building sites. In the 2000s, one of them was Bo Xilai, the charismatic ruler of Chongqing (see Chapter 4), who initiated a seemingly unironic fad for Mao-era propaganda karaoke. One hopes that such men (and they are mainly men) remember the awful excesses of the 1960s and take careful steps to prevent history repeating itself. But for some, surely, there is the ineffable temptation to put a convenient name and a face on the atrocity. Mao made us do it. It was all him. We just followed orders. The hardliners still glorify his bold decisions and brutal solutions. For the millions yet living, who persecuted their friends, denounced their families and attacked their neighbours in the 1960s, it is perhaps easier to maintain the idea that such atrocities were somehow his responsibility alone.

For foreign observers, who often have access to a fuller picture of the famines and purges of his era, Mao is a reminder of what can happen when mob rule takes over. For a worryingly large proportion of young Chinese, he is an avuncular, benign deity like a distant emperor, with little evidence readily available to refute such an image.

2

Opening up

Poverty is not socialism. To be rich is glorious.

Deng Xiaoping

The last years of the Mao era saw his colleagues fighting over the right to succeed him. Lin Biao, once his heir apparent and the driving force behind the Little Red Book, fell from grace and died in mysterious circumstances in a plane crash, possibly fleeing the country after a failed coup attempt. Meanwhile, increasingly sour relations with the Russians made it possible for the Chinese to seek a rapprochement with other foreign powers.

The 180-acre island of Zhenbao turned out to be the unexpected flashpoint. It was here, midstream in the Ussuri River on the border with the USSR, that Chinese and Soviet soldiers exchanged gunfire in March 1969. Largely forgotten today (and only restored to Chinese control in 1991), Zhenbao was a symbol to Mao that the Soviet Union was not above directly attacking its former partner. Under the old adage that the enemy of your enemy is your friend, China was better off seeking allies elsewhere.

Matters were made easier for the People's Republic by the landmark United Nations Resolution 2758, which stripped Taiwan (the 'Republic of China') of the Chinese seat on the UN Security Council and reassigned it to the PRC. It was no coincidence that 17 nations petitioned the UN to make this change on 15 July 1971, the same day that the US President Richard Nixon announced that he would be visiting Beijing the following February.

Nixon's visit had been carefully and secretly organized by the Chinese Premier, Zhou Enlai, and by Nixon's negotiator Henry Kissinger. Kissinger was a renowned proponent of realpolitik – the doctrine that favoured pragmatism in politics, regardless of the moral consequences. Although Nixon had run for office on an anti-Communist ticket, and received considerable political support from the Taiwan lobby of wealthy overseas Chinese, his decision amounted to a reversal of the status quo since 1949. There was only room for one China on the Security Council, and it was now decided, after more than two decades, that Taiwan had been occupying the seat 'unlawfully'. Taiwan, and its 21.8 million residents, were no longer represented at the United Nations, except implicitly by their enemy, the People's Republic.

Posterity remembers the iconic meeting of Nixon and Chairman Mao, although they only had a single one-hour chat shortly after Nixon's arrival in China. The bulk of his diplomatic consultations were conducted with Zhou Enlai, who was locked in a bitter struggle with Mao over the direction of the country. The visit resulted in the Shanghai Communiqué, the basis of Sino–American relations ever since, which included a joint declaration that neither country would 'seek hegemony in the Asia-Pacific'. It also stated that there was only 'One China', effectively shutting Taiwan out from any international summit, conference or even sporting event at which the People's Republic was present.

▶ Deng takes charge

As early as 1963, Premier Zhou Enlai had suggested, within the framework of Chinese Communism, that

▲ The importance of Nixon's visit to China was recognized globally, as seen in this commemorative stamp from one of the United Arab Emirates.

'Four Modernizations' would be required to ensure that progress continued at an acceptable pace. He regarded the key areas as agriculture, industry, national defence and science/technology. Although he got nowhere with this proposal, he would reintroduce it 12 years later, shortly before he succumbed to cancer. Zhou did so when he realized he had nothing left to lose, leaving a new generation, led by his protégé Deng Xiaoping, to undo the damage wrought by the Mao era.

Deng had been purged (twice) during the Cultural Revolution, but was pardoned and came back to Beijing, where he remained, at least on paper, a second-tier figure below the new Chairman, Hua Guofeng (1921–2008). When he did return to power, he negotiated a careful route through Party rhetoric in order to keep up appearances.

Deng's era was characterized by continued praise of Mao, and continued reverence to the Chairman's personality cult. But Mao's words were not, as they had been in the era of the Cultural Revolution, regarded as infallible dogma. Instead, they were parsed as shrewd reactions to situations of their time. This neatly preserved the idea of Mao as a great leader, while allowing his successors the option of changing their minds in the face of new conditions. What mattered to Deng Xiaoping was not so much 'what Mao would do' as the ability to spin any new decision as if it were.

Deng had travelled to France on a diplomatic mission in 1975, and returned boggled by how far behind China had fallen. Realizing that many Party cadres continued to agree with the propaganda because they knew no differently, he encouraged other opinion formers to see for themselves how the world now looked. This was largely aspirational in the mid-1970s, but became easier after the death of Mao had removed previous barriers to progress. By 1978, Deng felt secure enough to say the unthinkable, in an article for a southern Chinese newspaper: 'Recently our comrades had a look abroad. The more we see, the more we realize how backward we are.'

His comment reflected a general admission among the elite that Mao's self-assured leadership had gone far off course over the last 20 years. Many had endured the hardships of the Cultural Revolution in the belief that there was no alternative. Now, visits to the 'revisionist' Communist state of Yugoslavia, and even the old bugbears of the capitalist West had revealed that life was palpably better there, even for the working class, which would supposedly be downtrodden under capitalism. Perhaps the most persuasive discovery was just over the border in Hong Kong, where Chinese people under a foreign power seemed to be flourishing. Deng's administration capitalized directly on this by setting up an enclave snuggled up against Hong Kong itself, where foreign capital could buy cheap Chinese labour to assemble items for export. This was soon renamed the Shenzhen Special Economic Zone, and would become an icon of economic reform in the decade to come. Hong Kong itself became the focus of an initiative to strengthen trade and connections, as a waypoint between China and the rest of the world. Deng refused to believe that there was anything wrong with being rich – to him, the real ideal of Communism was that everybody would be rich. 'To get rich is glorious,' he said. 'It doesn't matter if some areas get rich first.'

▲ A propaganda poster from 1978, celebrating the 'Excellent Performance of the Chinese Communist Party'.

Deng signalled his resolve with a series of prominent visits to large manufacturing areas, where he reiterated his plans in ever-clearer terms. Away from the capital, he was able to bypass many controls on free speech that would have made it difficult for him to openly criticize Chairman Hua on his home turf. The economist Hu Fuming had captured the mood of the time with an article titled 'Practice is the Sole Criterion for Judging Truth' (1978); Deng had already summarized this, Mao-style, in more proverbial form: 'It doesn't matter whether a cat is black or white, as long as it catches mice.'

Post-WW2 Japan, reconstructing at a breakneck pace, was the new model, leading to the enthusiastic, ruthless adoption of foreign methods, injections of foreign capital and an overriding concentration on science and technology. Owing to periodic spats in Sino–Japanese relations, the role of Japan would often be subsequently downplayed; during the 1980s, when China was fervently copying a Japanese model, and Japan was the single largest source of investment in China, particularly in manufacturing, this fact often went unmentioned. However, like Japan, China carefully managed foreign contact, welcoming investment but keeping outsiders at arm's length through special government offices. In the 20th century, unlike the 19th century, foreign investment would not mean bowing to foreign pressure on religious or cultural matters.

Deng shrewdly chose to concentrate on areas that would see the swiftest material results for the Chinese man in the street. With cloth still rationed and no free agricultural land on which to grow cotton, he pushed for foreign investment in factories producing synthetic fibres, inadvertently jump-starting China's nylon fashion trends in the 1980s.

Deng noted the words of Mao himself, that the late leader's 'true spirit' was one of 'seeking the true path from facts' – in which case, surely it was time that the facts spoke for themselves? Conditions had changed, he said with exquisite care – Mao was right then; but if he were alive today, he would have changed his position to reflect these new facts. Mao's China had clung to a model inherited from the discredited Soviets; it was time for a change. Deng also played the self-criticism card, apologizing on behalf of the government for letting down the Chinese people in the past. It was phrased as a personal apology, albeit for the actions of others.

It was a quiet coup, since all parties knew that it would be dangerous to let either China or the outside world see that there was friction within the Party. Behind the scenes, Chairman Hua agreed to step aside, remaining as leader in name only, while Deng's words, issued as those of a mere 'vice premier', were increasingly reported as the official Party line. Such declarations included an opinion that would become the basic position on Mao himself: that China had benefited greatly from his leadership, but that he was not infallible. This equivocation on Mao is arguably what has kept him as a prominent icon today despite the discrediting of much of his later leadership.

▶ 'Socialism with Chinese characteristics'

In 1982, the communes that had dominated agriculture since 1958 were abolished. It was now regarded as 'socialist' for individual households to manage their own affairs, as they had done for thousands of years before Communism. Collective agriculture remained in some areas, particularly the northeast, where conditions favoured large-scale pooling of resources and manpower. But elsewhere in China, farming became a largely private enterprise.

Deng's favouring of chemical industries led to a vast increase in the availability of artificial fertilizers, allowing post-commune harvests to suggest that lessening controls on farming would lead to better productivity. Much to everybody's surprise, the grain harvest in 1984 was, genuinely, 25 per cent larger than the preceding year's. The government, which had previously bought all rice at a fixed rate, suspended this captive market, encouraging farmers to move into other crops and spurring an explosion in market gardening, with the emphasis on *market*. Some even turned from food to cash crops such as cotton and tobacco, reducing China's reliance on foreign imports. Others stuck to fruit and vegetables, swiftly improving the quality of food nationwide by competing on the open market. Peasants got wealthier, improving in turn their own conditions – with better resources came better tools and refrigeration, and with that, still higher quality, reach and monetization of produce.

Meanwhile, factories and workshops that had previously been inwardly focussed, serving only the needs of their specific commune, were now free not only to specialize in whatever they did best, but also to trade their products further afield. Money, which Mao had once tried to abolish altogether, now seemed to form a far better incentive to workers than the more general idea of serving the commune.

▶ State capitalism

If this all reads like propaganda for the benefits of capitalism, that's because it was. Deng's reforms seem to have begun as a temporary measure to alleviate the threat of famine. He confessed that he had been taken aback by the degree to which private enterprises, or as the Party carefully described them so as not to rock the boat, 'co-operatives', had 'spontaneously' sprung into being as a result.

There were several distinct factors within the Chinese economy that allowed it to develop so fast. Thousands of miles of sea coast allowed rapid development of sea trade – swifter to arrange, in the short term, than the building of more roads. Ethnically, millions of 'foreigners' in the US, Australia, Malaysia and elsewhere still counted themselves as being of Chinese descent, and could be leaned upon for investment. So, too, could Western capitalists lured by the thought of a population of a billion potential consumers for any new product.

The apparent success of this under-the-counter capitalism mattered to Party hardliners because it could all too easily have been a false dawn. The economy, cautioned one, was like a bird that could not be held in the hand, but still had to be caged or it would fly away. Everybody knew what capitalism was – Marx had, after all, written a whole book about it. It led to imperialism, inequality and corruption. It was Communism's unwelcome opposite – a false friend that offered trinkets and luxuries, while undermining the principles of a collective society. In Gorbachev's Russia, reforms were couched as anti-Communist, and did indeed bring down the Communist state. But Deng remained unwavering in his support of Communism in principle–withtheseeconomicexperimentsmerelydesigned to help the Communist state attain its longer-term goals. Nor did he copy Mikhail Gorbachev's sudden 'big bang' of reforms, instead leaving his Party apparatus in tandem with private enterprise.

Deng's reforms were the thin end of the wedge. Already, the surplus of food had removed the need for rationing, which in turn had removed controls that stopped many young rural Chinese from moving to the cities. Crime rates were rising as people began once more to distinguish between haves and have-nots, and cities began to gain a growing population that was euphemistically described as 'waiting for employment'. Deng suggested that some of these surplus labourers could be put to use running 'household enterprises', such as groceries, bakeries, restaurants and garages. But surely this would mean they became capitalists?

A bright spark found a loophole in *Das Kapital*. In one section, Marx had written of a man who exploited the labour of his eight employees. Creatively reading this as a benchmark for evil, it was suggested that someone with only *seven* employees would fall short of the line, particularly if the boss was not a remote factory owner, but rolled up his sleeves and got dirty on the shop floor himself.

When, inevitably, it was pointed out that some people had more than seven employees, Deng pointed out how ludicrous the line was. He noted that stalwarts of the Mao era saw any progress as subversive, and that they were the sort of people who thought that a farmer with three ducks was a socialist, but a farmer with five ducks was a capitalist. Although couched as a joke, it was chillingly close to many justifications for lynchings and murders during Mao's purges of supposed 'landlords'. Deng's pronouncements on the issue remained flippant because neither he nor his supporters were keen on officially debating it. An official debate meant the possibility, however remote, of a drastic reversal that would be sure to put off many entrepreneurs who remembered previous changes in policy. Instead, Deng vaguely suggested that the Party should give it a few years and see what happened. In 1987, the Party Congress slipped into its announcements the concession that a labour force of more than seven didn't seem to do any harm. Meanwhile, price controls were removed on certain items, such as tobacco and alcohol.

In retrospect, this is where Deng's utopian vision stumbled. Until the end of the 1980s, the Chinese public had arguably enjoyed all the benefits of capitalism with none of its costs. Suddenly, prices started to rise. Many industrial concerns, particularly those that had only flourished with state protection, crashed and burned in a truly competitive environment, swelling the ranks of the unemployed. The retail price index in 1988 was 18.5 per cent higher than the previous year – itself a conservative estimate of actual levels of inflation. With increasing public complaint, the Party erupted in a carnival of finger-pointing. But Deng, of course, was still not the figurehead. The incumbent Premier, Zhao Ziyang (1919–2005), became the fall guy for Deng's experiments, and a series of economic brakes attempted to roll back some of Deng's reforms. But restoring previous conditions required tax revenue, which was now reduced along with the reduction of enterprise.

▶ The 'one-child' policy

Deng's era also saw a growing concern over the sheer size of China, and the possibility of a demographic time bomb. The first rumblings of concern over China's population came in September 1963. Specifically, it was the *urban* population that worried the authorities, with a new policy of encouraging couples to marry later and have fewer children. This ran counter to the peasant-focussed rhetoric of Chairman Mao, who had formerly pushed for big families as a patriotic duty. It was not until 1979 that the state instituted a wide-ranging series of population control directives, collectively known in the West, somewhat misleadingly, as the 'one-child policy'.

Despite the implications of the name, there is no nationwide law restricting families to a single child. But in China's cities, parents have been strongly encouraged to have a single child, and must pay a substantial fine (200,000 yuan, around £20,000/US$30,000) for any infractions.

Out in the countryside, where farmers often still struggled on the poverty line, and the infrastructure failed to offer urban levels of health care, an only daughter would effectively doom her parents to a lonely old age with nobody to care for them. The policy was hence fudged, so that rural dwellers whose first child was a girl were allowed to try again for the son who would be sure to do his filial duty. Ethnic minorities, too, were allowed more children.

The 'one-child' policy effectively slowed China's ballooning population, although it would have side effects of its own. Children born in the 1980s and after were often characterized in the media as 'little emperors', raised without siblings, over-indulged by parents and grandparents and developing a sense of arrogant entitlement.

▶ From the Democracy Wall to Tiananmen

Deng suggested that 'the masses should be encouraged to offer criticism'. This was misinterpreted in some quarters as a call for freedom of speech. One icon of Deng's reforms was the so-called Democracy Wall, the name for a patch of brickwork near a busy central Beijing bus stop where poems, articles, posters and similar items critical of the regime began to appear in the 1970s. Some of the articles took the tone of a loyal opposition, pointing out, for example, that other Communist states were grappling with issues such as the rise of a new elite among the families of Party cadres.

Inevitably, the wall became a locus for more active protests. It became a site, not merely for posters, but for pamphleteers distributing more aggressive calls for reform, and ultimately a site of assembly for protesters, some of whom marched on the nearby Party headquarters in January 1979. The posters changed from earnest suggestions to strident attacks, including some upon the very foundations of Communism itself. Some visitors, such as the zookeeper Wei Jingsheng, who briefly became an international celebrity, openly called for a 'fifth' modernization from Deng: democracy itself. Wei's attack was particularly damaging, because it voiced a criticism that none had dared utter – that all the words, bluster and aspirational declarations of Communism had not removed the old inequalities; it had merely renamed them. Meanwhile people were still begging for food, dissidents were still being locked up, and the people were still not 'free'.

While the word 'democracy' appeared in Deng's speeches, and while the Democracy Wall had proved useful to him when he was opposing Hua Guofeng behind the scenes, it had outlived its usefulness. One Party grandee archly observed that Deng's attitude towards democracy was like that of a legendary prince who loved pictures of dragons, but was terrified by the arrival of a real one. Deng preferred to couch things in his usual homespun way: 'If you open the window, some flies will get in.'

By spring 1979, Deng had made his position clear – there was to be no media, of any kind, formal or informal, 'opposed' to the Party, Mao, Communism or its foundations. A scapegoat was required, and Wei Jingsheng fit the requirements, along with some 30 other prominent critics. They were arrested and chastized. The wall, meanwhile, was moved to a more out-of-the-way location, where would-be critics were now obliged to present ID before posting. In March 1979, even this pale shadow was shut down.

The Democracy Wall, initially welcomed, but abandoned in much the same way as the 'hundred flowers' campaign of the previous generation, was merely one of several oppositional movements of the early 1980s, in which the new generation of students was particularly vocal. Elements of unrest within China at that time included students demanding more 'democracy', as well as workers protesting about the economic reforms – some that they were proceeding too fast, others that they were not proceeding fast enough.

Deng's policies might have revitalized China, but they did so in a haphazard way. The 1980s were characterized by starts and stops, as Party hardliners periodically clamped down on the drift away from

Communism. Periodic campaigns against 'spiritual pollution' warned the people against an obsession with material goods. Conversely, Deng's insistence on the paramount importance of science and technology completely reversed the previous institutionalized hatred of intellectuals, restoring a nationwide respect for educational achievement. Inevitably, some of these new students brought up the subjects of the May Fourth Movement, and its demands for *two* new friends – Mr Science and Mr Democracy. Where, they asked, was the latter?

The protests achieved a new momentum in April 1989, when the reformer Hu Yaobang died. This prompted students to gather 'in mourning' in Tiananmen Square, which not even the hardest-hearted of Party officials could call unpatriotic. Of course, it also created a vibrant gathering on the eve of 4 May, the anniversary of the student protest that had begun it all back in 1919. By the end of May, the presence in the Square had grown into a massive, multi-leadered, multi-purposed mass of people.

Western historical memory usually characterizes these protesters as 'students', and indeed, many of them were. But similarly large numbers comprised workers laid off amid economic reforms, or protesting about corruption. Western journalists were swift to read the protests as a youthful call for liberalization, but many of those present in the Square were complaining *about* the liberalization already under way under Deng, which had cost them their jobs. Some of the hunger strikes among protesters were democracy-focussed, but others were intended to highlight the elaborate banquets and networking by modern Party officials, regarded by the more idealistic protesters as a form of corrupt, back-scratching graft – dining out on lavish expense accounts while elsewhere people starved.

Nor was Beijing the only site of protests. Similar demonstrations took place in large cities such as Wuhan, Xi'an, Nanjing and Guangzhou. When the infamous crackdown began, soldiers were deployed not only in Beijing, but also in Chengdu. But it's Beijing that got the attention, where embedded foreign journalists memorably documented the panic and terror as the army marched in to break up the event with tear gas. In Shanghai, the local mayor Jiang Zemin diffused protests without bloodshed but with heavy-handed media clampdowns – an unsung achievement that helped propel him into the running to be the next leader of China, untainted by the Tiananmen associations of many of his superiors.

The Tiananmen Square incident provided overseas Chinese with some of their most enduring icons, including the Goddess of Democracy, whose original representation lasted only a few days before being ripped down and pulverized. Designed as an artful combination of the Statue of Liberty and the many divine personifications of virtue to be found in Communist propaganda, this short-lived plaster lady has since been resurrected all around the world in multiple forms. She has been seen in pop-up installations in Taiwan and

Hong Kong, and in more enduring bronze forms in San Francisco, Vancouver, Washington, DC and several other North American cities.

Similarly iconic is the famous photograph of an anonymous figure, shopping bags incongruously clutched in his hands, facing down a row of tanks. The 'Tank Man' has come to symbolize much of the rhetoric of citizens standing up to a brutal government, although we might also note that the picture tells only part of the story. The tanks, which were heading *away* from the Square, had clearly stopped. Footage of the actual incident clearly shows the figure climbing on the tank and remonstrating with its occupants, but he remained unharmed. Two unknown figures eventually rushed from the crowd and dragged him off, and his whereabouts thereafter have been unknown.

All of the above, however, is only iconic *outside* China. The Tiananmen Square incident of 1989 is notable for its absence from media within China, where all photographs and discussion of it have been so thoroughly excised from the media and internet that, if it is known at all, it is known only as a rumour. Mention the Tiananmen Square protests to a modern Chinese citizen, particularly one born since 1989, and you are more than likely to find yourself talking about the outbreak of trouble in the square after the death of Zhou Enlai in 1976, or even the protests of 4 May 1919. 'Tiananmen' has become Western shorthand for the incident, but say the word to a PRC citizen, and they will usually assume you are talking about the Square itself.

民主女神 1989

▲ Replica of the 'Goddess of Democracy' created in Hong Kong as part of a 2013 protest marking the anniversary of the Tiananmen Square Incident.

▶ The Southern Tour

Jiang Zemin took power as the General Secretary of the Communist Party in 1989, amid the unrest following Tiananmen. The next few years were a period in which some came to question the wisdom of Deng's reforms, suggesting a return to the old values of the Mao era. Although Deng had officially resigned from his main posts, and suffered a loss of face after the Tiananmen crackdown, this made little difference to his political clout. He had, after all, never been the official leader of China, despite being described by many as 'paramount' for his influence on his colleagues and supposed superiors. Now plain old 'Comrade' or 'Uncle' Xiaoping, rather than a Party Chairman or even member of the People's Congress, he undertook a high-profile trip to China's prosperous south, in order to reiterate his goals for economic reform.

The Chinese press was not sure what to do about Deng's trip, and would only cover it in depth several months later. It would eventually be known as the Nanxun (Southern Tour), using terminology that had once been reserved for the inspections of far-flung parts of an emperor's domain. On his trip, Deng visited high-profile development zones like Shenzhen and Zhuhai, sites of many export-focussed factories, stating his support for economic reform, and his criticism of those who might try to put the brakes on.

You have to use a two-fisted approach. With one hand, you grab reform and openings. With the other, you grab every kind of criminal behaviour. You have to have a firm grip with both hands.

Deng Xiaoping, 1992

Deng's health was failing, he was already showing the early tremors of Parkinson's disease, but his trip was a calculated statement of his beliefs, calling for an 'opening-up' (*kaifang*). Jiang Zemin, a leader with very limited immediate support among the Party Congress, got the message, and continued with Deng's policies, dismissing claims that China risked a new revolution like the one that had recently toppled Soviet Russia.

▶ Deng matters

Deng Xiaoping matters because he did the unthinkable, steering a path through the minefield of Maoism to usher in a new age of prosperity. In ousting Mao's official successor, Hua Guofeng, Deng demonstrated that the mass of impressive job titles among the Party committee did not necessarily reveal who truly ran the country. But in removing Hua *peacefully*, Deng showed that it was possible to oust opponents without reprisals. The fallen Hua remained an obscure but active member of the government for another two decades, only retiring in 2002. Others were not so lucky, including Zhao Ziyang, who spent 15 years under house arrest.

Deng's new age was firmly couched in the rhetoric of 'socialism with Chinese characteristics'. He continues to matter because his reforms introduced a style of state capitalism that left the Party intimately and inextricably connected to the new industries and concerns. Most notably, the man who ushered in such sweeping economic reforms also unhesitatingly send troops into Tiananmen

▲ Deng Xiaoping supposedly discouraged the personality cult stylings of his predecessors, although he could still be seen on many billboards as a harbinger of future prosperity.

Square to contain protests. His behaviour over the Democracy Wall carries within it the seeds of the modern Chinese internet, where net café browsers must present their ID, and where Party scrutineers vet all content.

The degree to which today's Communist Party is actually *Communist* is debatable. But it is undeniably an elite, controlling force within Chinese society. In allowing the monolithic Party to make such radical changes in the name of its continued adherence to 'socialism' and the wishes of the masses, Deng preserved much of its legacy despite the disasters of the 1960s. His reforms brought riches to literally millions, although in a nation of over a billion, that still leaves much room for poverty. Although it may be 'glorious to get rich', there are millions who are still waiting, or struggling, for such an opportunity.

3

'One Country, Two Systems'

Hong Kong's star will continue to climb. Hong Kong's values are decent values. They are universal values. They are the values of the future in Asia as elsewhere, a future in which the happiest and the richest communities, and the most confident and the most stable too, will be those that best combine political liberty and economic freedom as we do here today.

Chris Patten

Hong Kong is a key to understanding changes in international policy, and in the power relationships between China and the rest of the world during the period in office of Deng's successor, Jiang Zemin. Among many communities of the Chinese diaspora, particularly in the English-speaking world, Hong Kong is a locale with strong ancestral or familial connections. Along with nearby Macau, a former Portuguese colony, it matters in radically different ways for the People's Republic of China, most pointedly as a diplomatic and political victory – a whole territory wrested back from the hands of Western imperialists without a shot being fired. It is also a political tool – a demonstration to the rest of the world, and most pointedly to Taiwan, that Communist China and capitalist ideals can co-exist without undue friction.

Hong Kong's 7 million people are only a tiny fraction of China's overall population, but are worth significantly more in economic terms – 13 per cent of the 'export' market for Chinese goods, and a major partner in many Chinese joint ventures. Hong Kong is not merely a market in its own right for Chinese material, but the engine that drives many factories and other businesses in south China, particularly in the Special Economic Zones of Shenzhen, Shantou and Zhuhai. China may have occupied Hong Kong, but there is an argument to be had that Hong Kong has also colonized much of China.

Once a possession of the British Empire, Hong Kong was 'returned' in 1997 to the People's Republic of China, an entity that did not exist at the time that the British took over the enclave. Hong Kong now exists in an odd state of limbo, officially part of China, but

▲ Hong Kong today is home to seven million people, with a GDP of $350 billion.

technically a foreign entity – with its own governmental system, currency and laws. Under the 1990 Basic Law, Hong Kong will retain this status until the year 2047, whereupon it will become fully integrated into whatever the People's Republic has become.

Hong Kong's status as a British colony was established in three treaties, of 1842, 1860 and 1898. The island of Hong Kong was, supposedly, ceded to Britain in perpetuity, although the New Territories on its northern edge were only granted in the final treaty on a 99-year lease. Following the Revolution, Chairman Mao officially rejected all 'unfair and unequal' treaties and deals signed by his forerunners, which could be taken as a tacit admission that Hong Kong was now British forever, just as China never contested the Pacific coast lost to Russia in 1858. Such a suggestion, however, was not good enough for the Hong Kong banking sector, members of which began to meekly enquire in the 1970s how they should progress with new 25-year development loans for the New Territories.

It was, it seemed, impossible to consider simply returning the New Territories, as they were integral to Hong Kong's entire infrastructure for power, water, residence and transport. Either Hong Kong was British for ever, or *all* of it would have to be handed back in 1997, when the New Territories lease ran out. In 1979, the Hong Kong governor Murray MacLehose put the question directly to Deng Xiaoping – there are still those in dark gentlemen's clubs who grumble that he should never have drawn attention to the issue. However, even in the unlikely event that the Chinese had previously forgotten the treaties, they would have been reminded of them in 1967, the year in which discussions first began with Portugal over the return of nearby Macau. In 1982, Deng officially stated China's interest in the return of Hong Kong, under mutually agreeable terms. Perhaps not without coincidence, his statement was issued the day after British forces took Port Stanley on the Falkland Islands, making abundantly clear the UK's foreign policy over matters of contested sovereignty.

▶ Poison pills

Until Taiwan was ousted from the UN Security Council, theoretically Hong Kong might have been 'returned' to the government in Taipei rather than Beijing. But with the PRC internationally established as the rightful ruler of China, it was firmly believed by many, including Deng himself, that this was a prelude to the end of the conflict between the 'two Chinas', and that within his own lifetime, the island of Taiwan would also rejoin the motherland. Deng did all he could to make this more likely, by warning the US off intensive arms supplies to the island, approving investment from Taiwan in China, encouraging direct links instead of the previous insistence on routes through third parties, and doing his best to set an example for how the Taiwan situation might also be handled.

> *If we can't reunify China right away, we will do it in a century; if not in a century, then in a millennium.*
>
> Deng Xiaoping

As for Hong Kong, Deng made life easier for the British by proposing 'One Country, Two Systems', a policy that would allow re-acquired pieces of Chinese territory (Hong Kong, Macau and, he added, even Taiwan) to continue to operate as capitalist economies – parts of China, but with the status of 'Special Administrative Regions.' True to Deng's political style, this was couched as a solution entirely within the bounds of the existing Chinese constitution, which already allowed the possibility of such enclaves. China would guarantee these new acquisitions relative autonomy for the following 50 years. This in turn led to a Sino–British Joint Declaration in 1984, later enshrined as the Basic

Law. In 1997, Hong Kong would be handed back to China, and life would go on as before.

Although it was a masterpiece of diplomacy, the negotiation over Hong Kong still created great controversy. Not the least aspect of this was the matter of the Hong Kong people themselves, whose nationality was bartered without consultation. Nor did the diplomats win many friends by enthusiastically announcing the handover of 6 million people into Chinese care mere months after tanks had been seen rolling across Tiananmen Square. Margaret Thatcher's government offered British passports to a mere 50,000 Hong Kong citizens who had grown up in the British dependency, leading many educated residents to seek nominal citizenship of more welcoming countries. This led to a sudden increase in immigration applications to the US, Canada and Australia, although many of these newly minted expats then returned to Hong Kong, secure in the knowledge that they could flee if matters took a turn for the worse. For those without bank accounts or academic qualifications as capital, any passport would do – consuls from Tonga, Ecuador and Gambia were soon rushing through passport applications, sometimes with questionable provenance.

Deng was worried that the British smiles might hide some other scheme. Was there, he wondered, a 'poison pill' lurking in their good-hearted handover? He fretted that the British would snap up so much real estate in Hong Kong that they would still effectively own it as landlords; that government salaries would be bumped up to silly levels, in order to make the Chinese look bad when they reduced them; or that they might find some other means of ripping the Chinese off.

▲ Both Deng Xiaoping and Margaret Thatcher regarded their negotiations over Hong Kong as a diplomatic victory.

▶ The Rose Garden

Hong Kong's last British governor was the pugnacious Chris Patten, an unseated Tory MP who whipped up some controversies of his own, possibly as the fall guy for schemes from higher up. In the wake of Tiananmen, Patten supported a new call for 'democracy' of some sort in Hong Kong. Although the people of Hong Kong had had little say in their own government for the previous 99 years of British rule, plans were afoot by 1991 to make the region's Legislative Council (LegCo) a democratically elected body. Current requirements for the president of LegCo is that he or she should be no less than 40 years old, a resident of Hong Kong of at least 20 years' standing, and a Chinese citizen *without* a foreign passport – thereby excluding many of the upper and middle classes who had sought dual nationality before the handover.

Patten also oversaw another scheme, initiated after Tiananmen by his predecessor. The Port and Airport Development Strategy (PADS), little discussed today, was a cunning plan designed to maintain confidence in Hong Kong as a global hub. With competition from nearby Shenzhen and Guangdong airports, Hong Kong's overcrowded Kai Tak airport risked falling behind in the 21st century and removing much of Hong Kong's international clout. This was answered with a plan for a massive new airport, Chek Lap Kok, on Lantau Island, which would not be subject to a midnight–06.00 curfew, and which would free up the existing airport site for redevelopment – in the middle of the city, Kai Tak was prime real estate. Moreover, the decommissioning of Kai Tak would remove height restrictions for buildings on several nearby hills.

However, simply building a new airport was not enough. Chek Lap Kok was so distant from the centre that it would require a high-speed rail link, the expense of which would be so great that it would also need to justify its existence by linking other areas such as the container terminals. These, in turn, would need to be upgraded with deeper basins, in order to make them accessible to bigger ships. The reader might already see in the PADS project an echo of the old story about sending the leopard to get the dog that was sent to retrieve the fox down a hole, with ever escalating costs and plans. However, the successful macro-scheme of PADS would ensure that Hong Kong would not become a backwater overshadowed by big

▲ Chek Lap Kok airport on Lantau Island was the centre of an intricate macro-development scheme to secure the colony's future and create thousands of jobs.

projects on the Mainland, and keep its international flavour. It would also, of course, require vast expenditure, allowing the British authorities to drain a hundred billion Hong Kong dollars from the local coffers. The money was often poured into the hands of construction companies with British, French and US ties. Some money made its way to Chinese companies, but often for low-tech work like dumping rocks in the sea to create landfill for the new runways.

The PADS scheme, also known as the Rose Garden Project (perhaps in the sense that 'we never promised you a...') had formerly been proposed and rejected because it would cost too much money. However, as a gesture of faith in an international Hong Kong, and a job creation scheme to stem the tide of emigration, it was a supremely bold and successful move. Completed in time for the Handover, it gave the Chinese a future-proof trading centre, while also siphoning off billions.

▶ Article 23

Since the Handover, Hong Kong has continued to debate and refine its constitution. The most controversial debate broke out in late 2002 over Article 23 of the Basic Law, which reads:

The Hong Kong Special Administrative Region shall enact laws on its own to prohibit any act of treason, secession, sedition, subversion against the Central People's Government, or theft of state secrets, to prohibit foreign political organizations or bodies from conducting political activities in the Region, and to prohibit political organizations or bodies of the Region from establishing ties with foreign political organizations or bodies.

On paper, this is little different from the situation under the British, when many foreign organizations, including both the Communist Party and the Kuomintang, were forbidden. Nor was it all that dissimilar to certain other nations' tightening of 'homeland security' issues in the wake of the 9/11 terrorist attacks a year earlier. The Secretary of Security, Regina Ip, who was later forced to resign over the issue, argued that it was merely a natural part of the process of integration with China, and reflected Beijing's desire to bring Hong Kong's administration closer into line with laws in the rest of the country.

However, attempts to implement Article 23 in the form of a new 'anti-subversion' law were met with strong protests. Part of the problem was that the law, drafted in the style of the PRC, did not distinguish between the one-party 'country' of China and the democratically elected 'government' of Hong Kong. Opposing the government in any form, even by standing against an incumbent in an election, could now technically be interpreted as opposing the country, and hence seditious. Meanwhile, the authorities could now define what constituted inflammatory or seditious acts of speech. If one wanted to apply the exact letter of the newly proposed law, it would become a crime not only to utter 'instigatory' words, but also to hear them without reporting them to the authorities. Moreover, this law was expected to apply not only to Hong Kong citizens, but also to any visitors, who might, in extreme circumstances face imprisonment for merely hearing a stranger say something that the authorities defined as seditious. In the event of such a situation, the police would not need a warrant to arrest them!

▲ A bauhinia, or 'Hong Kong orchid', forms the basis of the emblem for the Special Administrative Region.

In the scheme's defence, the President of Hong Kong's executive, Tung Chee-hwa, claimed that journalists would still have freedom of speech, as long as their words were in 'the public interest'. After all, Article 28 of the Basic Law still guaranteed that:

No Hong Kong resident shall be subjected to arbitrary or unlawful arrest, detention or imprisonment.

Arbitrary or unlawful search of the body of any resident or deprivation of the restriction of the freedom of the person shall be prohibited. Torture of any resident or arbitrary or unlawful deprivation of the life of any resident shall be prohibited.

The new law, however, left the definition of 'lawful', and indeed of 'public interest' in the hands of the authorities.

The proposed changes to Article 23 were eventually dropped, after peaceful protests in Hong Kong, and also after several local banks threatened to relocate, fearing the implications for the free flow of information. Commentators, including the visiting British Prime Minister Tony Blair, were quick to suggest that this reversal was democracy in action, and that the system was functioning precisely as it should. Across the water in Macau, a similar Article 23 was successfully implemented, albeit with a few alterations seemingly inspired by the objections in Hong Kong.

▶ Taiwan

Deng Xiaoping's plans for 'One Party, Two Systems' to also apply in Taiwan were thwarted, at least in his lifetime. Proposals in 1979 for three direct links – of post, transport and trade – were rebuffed by Chiang Kai-shek's son and heir, Chiang Ching-kuo, with the 'Three Nos': no contact, no compromise, no negotiation. However, with the death of Chiang in 1988, Deng genuinely appeared to believe that Taiwan would soon follow Hong Kong, that is, as soon as it was established that the people of Hong Kong were safe in Chinese hands. He even suggested that the status quo could continue on Taiwan for 'as long as a thousand years', if the island would only officially return to the fold as a Special Administrative Region. That, however, was not going to happen. The Nationalists would never bow to Communist pressure – and still occasionally spouted rhetoric that implied the Communists should bow to *them*. Meanwhile, the lifting of martial law in Taiwan, and the relatively swift arrival of a multi-party democracy soon afterwards, tied up the island in new wrangling over what to do with its freedom to choose.

▲ There is little on the surface today to distinguish Taiwan from any other part of China, but political rifts still run deep.

Certainly, there are realists in Taiwan who see that, economically and culturally, the island is already firmly tied to the Mainland. However, Nationalist hardliners will never proclaim what is in effect a conditional surrender to the Communists. Meanwhile, a new faction has arisen in Taiwan, championing the cause of the island's aboriginal inhabitants, and arguing that a Taiwan free to choose its destiny should proclaim itself to be independent. Ronald Reagan, while running for election as US president, did not help matters by openly suggesting that 'Taiwan is a country', and as such deserved to have its separate diplomatic relationship with the US. Those are fighting words to the Communists, who have tolerated Taiwan's de facto independence for 50 years, but have threatened to invade if the island that is still officially 'part of China' were to secede.

It is likely, over the *next* 50 years, that these arguments will matter less and less. China and Taiwan already resemble one another economically. There is a powerful hybridity of popular culture, particularly visible in music, literature, TV and fashion. Taiwan offers something of an outlet for Mainland discontents, and is a rich source of investment for Chinese firms. We should not downplay the deep-seated convictions that keep the two nations divided; equally, we should not ignore the powerful cultural incentive to make ties ever stronger.

In 1995, Jiang Zemin issued a proclamation to the effect that China would never tolerate an independent Taiwan. However, a Taiwan with stronger connections to the Mainland, in all senses but the political, seems to appeal to those on both sides of the Strait. In the early 21st century,

China has ceased to talk of reunification, and Taiwan has ceased to talk, at least not quite so loudly, of independence – seemingly a pact between the two. Jiang's own statement alluded to another issue, stating that military action would be unlikely as long as foreign powers remained neutral in any discourse between the two Chinas.

From Jiang Zemin's 'Eight-Point Proposal' – 30 January 1995

We shall try our best to achieve the peaceful reunification of China, since Chinese should not fight Chinese. We do not promise not to use force. If used, force will not be directed against our compatriots in Taiwan, but against the foreign forces who intervene in China's reunification and go in for 'the independence of Taiwan'. We are fully confident that our compatriots in Taiwan, Hong Kong and Macau and those residing overseas would understand our principled position.

▶ Tibet

Infamously, the other place in China that enjoys special status is Tibet, that mountainous region that stretches from the edge of Sichuan to the Himalayas and India. Since 1722, not long after the start of the Qing dynasty, Tibetans had been left to manage their own affairs under Chinese suzerainty, with the Chinese managing foreign affairs. Frictions developed at the time of the Qing dynasty's fall in 1911, which Tibet saw as a chance to claim full independence, and which the new Republic of

China refused to allow. Relations between Tibetans and the Chinese worsened in the 1950s when those Tibetans living outside Tibet proper, in provinces such as Sichuan and Gansu, objected to attempts to drag them into the reforms, collectivizations and cultural experiments of the Mao era. These protests spread to Tibet itself, and eventually led to Chinese clampdowns and the flight of Tibet's theocratic ruler, the Dalai Lama, to India in 1959. Tibet, like every other region with any sense of difference, such as the Autonomous Prefectures of Uyghurs, Kazakhs and Kyrgyz in Xinjiang, suffered particularly during the Cultural Revolution, when Red Guards singled out its traditional religious infrastructure for particular abuse.

As a result, repairing relations with the Tibetan Autonomous Region was a problem contemporary with the negotiations over the return of Hong Kong and Macao. Deng Xiaoping, however, noted publicly that it was naïve of the Dalai Lama to act as if he were the head of an independent state. With 80,000 Tibetans in exile in India and likely to influence the Dalai Lama's policy statements, Deng attempted to demonstrate that conditions in Tibet had improved under Chinese rule. However, visiting delegates were only impressed by crowds demonstrating in *support* of the Dalai Lama, and not by the treatment of Tibetans by the Chinese. Moreover, the Tibetans continued to demand the 'return' of conditions that had not even existed under the Qing dynasty – not only an independent Tibetan state, but also the expansion of its borders to include those parts of neighbouring provinces with large Tibetan populations – vestiges of medieval times, when Tibet had been far larger, and controlled areas of territory now considered 'Chinese'.

Meanwhile, Chinese settlers surged into Tibet, following tax breaks and incentives introduced in the third quarter of the 20th century. Members of other ethnic minorities sought to capitalize on Tibetan subsidies in the 1990s by also moving there. At the end of the century, rural communities remained strongly Tibetan, but non-Tibetans threatened to crowd out the locals in the capital, Lhasa. Similar conditions have arisen in other western Chinese regions that were once dominated by China's 100-million strong ethnic minority population, now swamped by colonists from the Chinese majority.

▲ The Potala Palace, Lhasa, is a symbol of Tibet's unique and distinct culture, but the region has been under Chinese suzerainty for more than three centuries.

Arguably, the foreign connections that proved so valuable to Hong Kong have had the reverse effect in Tibet, where a vocal community in exile continues to push for a 'Free' Tibet, not a political reality since the late 17th century or arguably even before, and a 'Greater' Tibet – a state that has not existed since the 9th century AD. For as long as the exiles make literally medieval demands on the Chinese government, a compromise is unlikely. Meanwhile, Tibet becomes progressively less Tibetan, as new settlers continue to crowd out the locals. Anti-colonial arguments common all over the world, about the oppression of native peoples or the stamping-out of a unique ethnic lifestyle, gain additional traction in discussions of Tibet, which often see the Han Chinese as an occupying power. Tibet is a region strongly defined by religious belief and practice, under a regime in which 'superstition' is banned and an exiled religious leader also enjoys temporal influence. Organizations such as Free Tibet argue that Chinese dominion makes it impossible for native Tibetans to exercise their basic human rights – how can Tibet be 'autonomous' if its masters directly or indirectly dismantle its religious infrastructure? This matters, of course, deeply to the Tibetans, but it may also come to matter to sizeable populations of other religious believers. China's population of Christians is hard to count, but may be ten times the size of the population of Tibet. China's population of Muslims is estimated at 20 million. The Tibet issue matters not only to the Tibetans, but as an indicator of how any other 'different' group might find accommodation with the power of a Party that denies religion, but believes in Marx and Mao.

▶ Jiang matters

'One Country, Two Systems' can still lead to tension. In an incident caught on a phone camera in January 2012 and inevitably uploaded to the internet, a Mainland girl dropped some noodles on the Hong Kong metro. A fellow passenger protested to the girl's family, and was forced to do so in halting Mandarin, as none of the visitors spoke Cantonese. As an argument broke out between them and other passengers, one woman shouted that there was no point in trying to reason with such yokels. 'Noodlegate' was soon parsed as an example of a wider malaise, in which Mainland Chinese were disparaged as uncouth 'locusts' that leeched off Hong Kong's thriving infrastructure, while the Hong Kong people were caricatured in turn as snooty 'lap dogs' of capitalism, clinging to the mannerisms and standards of their former imperialist masters. It became a *cause célèbre* in the Chinese media, as a reflection of the underlying tensions between differing classes, income groups or even ethnicities to be found in many parts of China.

Jiang Zemin, the General Secretary of the Communist Party from 1989 to 2002, was once cruelly known as 'the Flowerpot' in his Shanghai days, supposedly because was visible but served no real function. He inherited Deng Xiaoping's legacy, and chose to continue it, despite the collapse of Communist regimes elsewhere in the world. He did so by refusing to connect economic prosperity with calls for democracy, reinforcing the Party's intimate involvement in state capitalism, and brooking no alternative. Jiang's crackdowns on dissent were instrumental post-Tiananmen, but perhaps most visible in his campaign against the Falun Gong religious cult, which had arranged a mass protest outside Party headquarters, and which he branded as a threat. In his blunt, dismissive exercise of power against dissent, we see the first stirrings of the 'harmonious society' that would be implemented by his successor (see next chapter).

Jiang faded fast from public view after the handover of his power to his successor Hu Jintao, largely because he lost his hold on the media. However, he shrewdly put many political cronies into mid-level positions before stepping down. A decade later, when Xi Jinping took over, Jiang Zemin was conspicuous at the front and centre – the bulk of the statesmen put into high office in 2012 were his appointees, now promoted to positions of political influence. The Flowerpot, it seems, understood how to nurture his plants.

4

The Games begin

The Beijing Olympic Games has promoted the Olympic spirit of solidarity, friendship and peace. It has become a grand event of international sports competition and cultural exchanges witnessed and joined by people of the whole world.

Hu Jintao

The period in office of Hu Jintao, General Secretary of the Communist Party from 2002 to 2012, saw China reach new heights in the international community. In 2001, the same year that China joined the World Trade Organization, it won the right to host the 2008 Olympics, chiefly in Beijing, ushering in a new period of high-profile visibility – China faced increased scrutiny and criticism over many elements of its society. These issues have sometimes been quietly addressed, and sometimes bluntly rebuffed, as the ruling Party seeks to maintain its hold on domestic power without compromising its rising international profile. Hu's signature philosophy throughout his period in power was one of a 'Socialist Harmonious Society' – a term that evoked ancient wisdom from Confucius, but came to imply harmony imposed by force, if necessary.

China's strategy for the Olympics began as early as 1990, when the country spent $300 million on hosting the Asian Games. By 1993, China was bidding to host the 2000 Olympics, although the International Olympic Committee (IOC) seemed unimpressed by the suggestions, for example, that China could guarantee a trouble-free Olympics *because* it was an authoritarian state. The failed bid attracted a list of things that needed to be fixed – international travel connections, telecommunications, and more English-speakers in the capital, all of which were dealt with in the next few years. So, too, were great swathes of Beijing's old town, with Mao-era slums and Qing-era hutongs bulldozed to make way for modern skyscrapers. In order to save face in the event of a second failure, much of these beautifications were undertaken in supposed preparation for the 50th anniversary celebrations of Mao's 1949 declaration of the People's Republic. It was only two years later that the alterations were put to their true purpose, impressing the returning IOC enough to win the 2008 bid.

The Olympics opened with a controversy seen at the time as symbolic of China's underhand management of its image, when the girl who sang 'Ode to the Motherland' at the opening ceremony was later revealed to have been lip-synching to the voice of a less photogenic performer. However, it has since transpired that many previous Olympic events had featured pre-recordings, including the entire performance of the Sydney Philharmonic in 2000.

> The Beijing Olympics and the Shanghai World Expo show just how much effort China is willing to spend to enter the global stage. But while China desires to understand the world, it fails to accept its universal values.
>
> *Ai Weiwei*

▲ On the auspicious eighth day of the eighth month, 2008, the opening of the Beijing Olympics attracted the attention of the global media.

▶ SARS and H1N5

Such a knee-jerk reaction to China's management of the media is only to be expected after the scandals of the intervening years, most notably the outbreaks of dangerous diseases on Chinese territory. Severe Acute Respiratory Syndrome (SARS) is now thought to have first appeared in Guangdong Province in November 2002, when a patient from a remote farm died from a virus that caused a high fever and breathing problems similar to pneumonia. Scientific evidence strongly suggests that the disease originated in bats, and somehow jumped across species, probably in the close confines of a south Chinese market.

Late that month, a Canadian disease-monitoring service, affiliated to the World Health Organization (WHO), picked up signs of a 'flu outbreak' in south China. The Chinese authorities, however, were slow to act on WHO requests for further information, such that by the time the news was official in February 2003, there had already been 500 fatalities, and the disease had spread beyond south China to Hong Kong, other parts of East Asia, and several other countries linked by air traffic. The strongest evidence arrived from Vietnam, where a Hong Kong plane was forced to land so a passenger could receive treatment for severe flu-like symptoms. Dr Carlo Urbani, the Italian physician who treated the patient, identified SARS as a dangerous disease requiring extreme preventative measures. His report, which triggered a WHO response that may have saved millions of lives, was delivered shortly before he himself was killed by the disease.

The 2003 SARS panic shut down or relocated many international conferences and sporting events. The virus was most deadly to the elderly, killing 10 of the infected, whose numbers were estimated at roughly 5,300 in China (349 deaths), 1,700 (299 deaths) in Hong Kong and another 1,000 (125 deaths) in foreign countries. Although isolation and prevention kept the virus from becoming a true pandemic, it was widely agreed that it had been a very close call, and that China's reluctance to share information had cost lives. The subsequent 2005 H1N5 'bird flu' and 2009 H1N1 'swine flu' scares were also suspected to have been the result of hygiene or sewage issues in southern China, particularly the management and storage of poultry, with which humans or domestic animals are far more likely to come into contact than wild birds.

Complaints about China's management of the news have associated China directly with the diseases, although this is unfair. The first recorded case of bird flu, for example, which dates from 1959, was in Scotland. China's overloaded health care system may itself cause a certain lack of transparency, but it is widely believed that China's failure to act quickly had more to do with a perceived loss of face, and with general restrictions on the freedom of information in China.

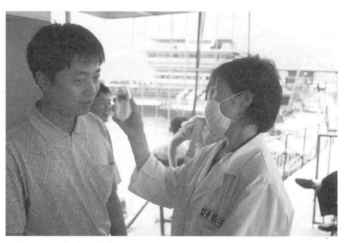

▲ Spot checks for high temperature became commonplace at airports in the wake of the SARS scare.

▶ The 'Great Firewall'

Most notorious is the 'Great Firewall', a catch-all term coined in 1997 by Geremie Barmé in *Wired* magazine for a series of internet censorship initiatives so thorough as to justify the consideration of the 'internet' and the 'Chinanet' as two separate entities. Largest among these is the venture known in China since 1998 as Golden Shield, which employs tens of thousands of internet monitors, human and automated, to shut down sites using forbidden words and search terms. Golden Shield's mission is supposedly to protect state security, the public interest and children from harmful and/or illegal data – pornography, computer viruses and anti-Chinese propaganda, but also dissenting views, publicity for banned organizations and foreign websites devoted to Chinese hot-button issues. Browsing the internet in China is certainly a very different experience from browsing it abroad, with many well-known news sites either entirely unavailable or frustratingly slow to load. In many cases, such as Facebook, the international version is unavailable, but local equivalents are offered that are easier for the Party to police, in a phenomenon termed by writer Michael Anti (a pseudonym for the banned blogger Zhao Jing) 'block and clone'. It remains possible for Chinese netizens to see the outside internet world by using a proxy server, but for the average user, the outside world only arrives on government-approved pages.

From 2005, Hu Jintao's government pushed a new buzzword, *hexie* (harmony). The simple, innocuous term has come to symbolize many aspects of Chinese society, from exhortations to respect one's neighbours, to attempts to eradicate social inequalities. It also became a Newspeak euphemism for any attempt to coerce people. It spawned a Chinese internet meme, in which harmony was deliberately written with the 'wrong' characters. It was still pronounced *hexie*, but was written with characters meaning 'river crab', and led to numerous in-jokes among the twittering classes about censors 'crabbing' malefactors. In an outpouring of cheeky caricatures, river crabs became poster-creatures of the Chinese internet, often depicted with tiny hammers and sickles as claws. They are still sometimes depicted in conflict with a non-existent breed of alpaca or llama, the cao ni ma ('grass mud horse'), whose name is a homonym for 'f*ck your mother' in Chinese, and has come to symbolize online dissent.

In the most widespread incident of crab-related imagery, an ill-fated attempt by the state to introduce compulsory nanny software on all Windows PCs was met with a tide of crustacean protest. The unfortunately named Green Dam Youth Escort, originally planned as pre-installed software, but eventually bundled for voluntary use, came with a pre-loaded and updatable list of forbidden websites, and a charmingly idiosyncratic feature that counted the number of pink-coloured pixels on screen, and shut down the image if they climbed above a certain level. While this certainly protected the internet browsers of China from stumbling upon images of Caucasian pornography, it also banned China's web surfers from looking at pictures of pigs.

The Chinese internet community was swift to protest in an oddly creative way, knocking up images of a manga-style heroine called Lu Ba Niang (the Green Dam Girl). Clad in a quasi-military uniform with an ironically short skirt, Lu Ba Niang patrolled the web with a paintbrush for censoring, and a red armband that read 'Discipline'. Her perky little hat was sometimes shown with a small crab insignia, while her misadventures soon included eroticized inspections of other cartoon characters, earnest propaganda songs about her desire to 'harmonize' the whole planet and fake stills from non-existent adventure games and cartoon shows, in which Lu Ba Niang attempts to bleed the fun from any situation with the misguided enthusiasm of a cartoon Red Guard.

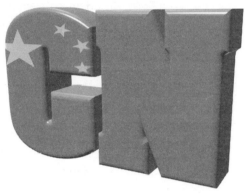

▲ Critics have argued that China's control over web access effectively divides the world into an Internet and a 'Chinanet'.

The Party, however, seems more than well aware of the power the internet offers for social action, particularly in a nation where 140 characters is enough to write a small essay, not merely a soundbite. Michael Anti has suggested that internet flash mobs can serve a similar function today to the Red Guards of the Cultural Revolution, unleashed to comment and kvetch in such overwhelming numbers that the Party can then be seen to be acting in 'response' to a mass line. When Sichuan was devastated by an earthquake in 2008, the Chinese microblogging sphere became the epicentre of a massive movement of charitable donations. This was, however, at least partly the result of peer pressure, as some donors were publicly berated for not giving enough. Charity, in the wake of the earthquake, was no longer voluntary, but defined by a form of mob rule. Similarly, a Party traffic official was ousted in Xi'an in 2012, when net users shared a photograph of him at the scene of an accident wearing an ostentatious Rolex. Unaffordable at his pay grade, this was regarded as an indicator of corruption, but it worryingly echoes the witch-hunts of the Mao era.

▶ The cake debate

One prominent and oft-discussed threat to 'harmony' has been the rise of China's new middle class, creating a large gap between rich and poor. Regionalism has risen again, not expressed in terms of independence and secessionism, but in terms of the economics of development, with cities like the 23 million-strong metropolis around Shanghai enjoying larger populations and economies than some foreign nations.

Bo Xilai, the controversial Party Secretary of Chongqing from 2007 to 2012, was one of the most flamboyant and recognizable of Chinese political figures, and was on a trajectory to become China's most outspoken and colourful new leader, before he was brought down by a colossal scandal. It was Bo who was responsible for the 'Sing Red, Strike Black' campaign in Chongqing, which encouraged a resurgence in the earnest Communist propaganda songs of years gone by – toe-tappers about patriotism, socialism and collective ethics, phased out of popular culture during the Deng Xiaoping era. In encouraging these Red Songs, coupled with his anti-crime campaign (Strike Black) that sought to root out corruption, Bo alluded to himself as the inheritor of old-school Communist traditions.

As the ruler of a municipality with a population of some 28 million people, Bo became embroiled in a war of words with his colleague Wang Yong, the Party Secretary of Guangdong province, over the amount of development funds being spent on the southern province, whose border with Hong Kong had made it a centre for new industries. Bo argued that it was time for regions beyond the mushrooming south to get a bigger slice of the cake. Wang countered that developments in Guangdong were to the benefit of all, and that he was, in effect, making a 'bigger cake'. Their great cake debate was seen by the Chinese media as a reflection of contending attitudes in modern China, with Bo speaking on behalf of old-school socialism for the benefit of all, while Wang was much more of a free-market advocate in the spirit of Deng Xiaoping, suggesting that it was better for some to get rich first, in order that everyone might eventually reap the rewards. Bo's argument might have held sway, but with his indictment on corruption charges, and his wife's conviction for murder, this champion of the new left might reasonably be said to have lost the argument.

▶ The food chain

The dairies of Inner Mongolia now form a powerful lobby in the Chinese supermarket sector. Adverts selling milk products are all over the place, and pushily insist on a number of bespoke varieties – this one for stronger bones, that one for more energy. They are so pro-active because Chinese parents have largely given up feeding Chinese milk to their children, after major scandals in the early 21st century. Chinese milk is probably the safest it has ever been, but public trust is at an all-time low.

In 2004, 16 Chinese children died of malnutrition after they were fed a 'milk formula' that turned out to be nutritionally worthless. This was no manufacturing error, but a deliberate scam that cruelly led several families to literally starve their own children to death, while believing that they were feeding them.

In 2007, a new problem arose, not over what was missing, but what was being added, when pet deaths in America were traced to melamine in the food chain, which had entered into Chinese pet food through contaminated animal feed. The size of the problem was difficult to judge without a national veterinary database, but in addition to the 14 confirmed pet deaths, several thousand were reported. It was claimed that mixing melamine into animal feed had been common practice for years, in the mistaken belief that there were no ill effects. Many animals were butchered before they died of renal failure from melamine poisoning, but this only delayed the discovery until it built up further along the food chain. Extensive testing found melamine in hundreds of food products for both pets and people, leading the Food and Drug Administration and the Department of Agriculture to estimate that up to 3 million Americans might have, for example, eaten chickens that had been reared on contaminated feed. Chinese food exports – of chicken, powdered egg and wheat gluten – were found to be similarly tainted.

Back in China, the food chain was discovered to be directly contaminated, when the budget dairy Sanlu was accused in November 2008 of selling a milk powder product that had been adulterated with melamine in an attempt to show higher protein levels. This may well have made the milk seem healthier, but it directly affected the health of some 300,000 people, many of them children in low-income families. Six children died of renal failure, while the original whistleblower, an employee at Sanlu who had been querying production standards since 2006, was later found stabbed to death in mysterious circumstances. A subsequent Chinese investigation found similar contamination in the products of 22 Chinese companies, causing a massive crisis of confidence, particularly among Chinese mothers. It is now far more common for Chinese mothers to feed their children exclusively on a diet of foreign milk formula, often sourced from Germany or New Zealand. Ironically, a New Zealand company, Fonterra, had owned a 43 per cent stake in Sanlu, and had requested a recall on suspect products eight months before the scandal broke. The deadly delay was blamed on mismanagement at a local level, as Chinese employees tried to save face by avoiding a public announcement of any danger.

▲ A series of scares and scandals has made Chinese parents reluctant to feed their children domestic milk formula, causing shortages as far away as the UK.

▶ The privileged elites

On 16 October 2010, a 22-year-old drunk driver knocked down two women on the campus of the University of Hebei. When local security guards rushed to the scene of the accident, he yelled at them that their mission was doomed, with the immortal words: 'Charge me if you dare. My dad is Li Gang!'

Of the 149,594 Li Gangs in China, the father in question was the public security chief. While he might conceivably have pulled a few strings to get his wayward son out of trouble for a parking offence or jaywalking, Li père was in no position to help here, particularly when one of the victims died in hospital. After a tearful apology on television, the driver was sentenced to six years in prison, but the incident served to highlight a growing sense of social inequality. Although Li Qiming paid for his crime, he had initially assumed that his connections would somehow get him off the hook, in an attitude alarmingly common among the two groups of 'elite' Chinese.

One is referred to as the 'princelings' (*taizi dang*), and comprises the families of Party grandees. Six decades after the proclamation of the People's Republic, some in the press have been heard to grumble that the children and grandchildren of revolutionaries are impossibly privileged 'Red boomers', and risk forming a new class of monopoly capitalists. Such accusations are nothing new, and indeed repeat terminology and complaints found as early as the 1930s. But Li Peng's children run two massive electric power companies; thanks to government contracts, Hu Jintao's son's company makes most of the luggage scanners in China; Mao Zedong's grandson is a major-general; Jiang Zemin's son became vice-dean of the Academy of Sciences. Perhaps they are really hardworking and smart, but their personal successes surely play havoc with a national belief in meritocracy and fairness. Sometimes, these 'princelings' are inadvertent pawns in their elders' power games, elevated to offices by others in order to curry favour with their parents. Wasn't the revolution supposed to put a stop to nepotism and privilege? But nor can they all go back to being peasants and miners... can they?

However, perhaps we should not be too quick to write off simple inheritance and opportunity as 'corruption'. There is far greater evidence of political 'dynasties' in, say, America, Japan or Taiwan than in the People's Republic of China, where no two heads of state have ever been related to each other by blood.

A similar group, simply comprising the children of rich Chinese without Party affiliations, is often called the 'wealthy second generation' (fu er dai). Many of them are the children of those Chinese who were brave, or foolhardy, enough in the early 1990s to 'jump into the sea' (xia hai), a leap of faith that Deng's transformation, Deng's promises, Deng's embrace of capitalism would somehow be a long-term proposition. These new oligarchs walked away from safe government jobs and state sinecures and risked everything on commerce. A generation later, their children are just that – kids with rich parents, who have known nothing but the good life. Wealth is also the easiest means of getting around the one-child policy, since for the rich, a 200,000-yuan fine per extra child is costly but not insurmountable.

A subject of some fascination and a certain degree of aspirational envy in modern China, this second generation is little different from the rich kids of any other country, known for their love of foreign brands, fast cars and conspicuous consumption. The fu er dai attracted the attention of the foreign media on foreign soil, when several of them were arrested by Vancouver police for illegally racing expensive muscle cars. Sports cars seem to form an integral part of China's nouveau riche mythos, particularly since a notorious crash in March 2012, in which a Ferrari 458 Spider was totalled on Beijing's Fourth Ring Road. The identity of the driver, who was killed instantly, was hushed up for several weeks, but eventually revealed as Ling Gu, the playboy son of a leading official. Conflicting reports suggested that he, and one of his two female passengers, was naked at the time.

All of which inevitably leads to the question – if Party politicians earn only £6,000/US$9,000 a year, how can their children be driving cars worth a quarter of a million? Similar questions were asked after the infamous public ousting of Bo Xilai, whose son was found to be studying at a foreign university far too expensive for his father's meagre pay packet. Bo junior was later revealed to be on a fully paid scholarship (American universities being more than prepared to cosy up with the son of the next possible leader of China), but such tales of lavish privilege sit badly with a supposedly meritocratic society.

▶ The one in ten

In 2008, a Muslim balloon seller in Tibet became the epicentre of a wave of unrest that led to rioting. A passing Tibetan father and son decided to buy one of his balloons, but as the balloon was handed over, *someone's* grip slipped. As the balloon floated serenely away, the seller demanded three yuan (about 30p/50¢). The father refused to pay for a balloon he didn't have, and a fight broke out. When the police arrived, they favoured the Muslim migrant worker, causing the largely Tibetan crowd to complain of favouritism. Before the night was over, the incident had escalated into a full-on demonstration, complete with rock-throwing monks.

It is a story repeated elsewhere – there are premonitions here of Hong Kong's Noodlegate. Political activists might see in it an indicator of the pecking order among China's minorities, particularly in Tibet. But there is a simpler, more prosaic reality on display here, too. Citizens on the margins are travelling long distances to scrabble for pennies; desperate individuals are risking their lives for their next meal.

Since the 1950s, Chinese law has restricted the movement of all its citizens. The rigmarole and form-filling usually required for a foreign visa is also required for any Chinese citizen who wishes to reside away from his or her hometown. Originally designed to keep agricultural labourers tied to their farmland, this 'hukou' system lost some of its force in the 1980s, when Deng Xiaoping's reforms and agricultural lay-offs seemed to all but encourage citizens to drift towards the growing cities.

The precise number of China's 'floating population' (*liudong renkou*) is difficult to determine, since many of them are illegal residents. However, conservative estimates suggest that some 120 million migrant workers have left their hometowns, either to work in nearby towns or to seek their fortune further afield. This amounts to the largest population movement in human history, bigger than the Jewish diaspora, the mass migrations of the Huns and Mongols – the barbarian incursions that did for the Roman Empire – or Stalin's forcible relocations of entire nations. Many migrants have the requisite paperwork and hence legal right of abode in their new home. But many millions are stuck in the wainscot of Chinese society, deprived of health care or social security, confined to 'hot-bed' shared dorm accommodation or at the mercy of gang masters. There is, in fact, a very real risk that, without reform of the Chinese system, a substantial proportion of urban Chinese will be disenfranchised by 2020, semi-legal city-dwellers, creating something akin to the 'proletariat' that Marx predicted would form the basis of a revolution.

The visitor to China soon encounters them, huddled at hotel entrances selling fans and postcards, hawking ethnic foods in back alleys or pestering tourists to buy knock-off Louis Vuitton handbags. Their cries are as familiar a part of modern China as The East is Red – a patois of broken trader's English like something from 19th century pulp fiction: 'Hey lady. Lookee-lookee. You wanna bagger? Watchee? Laser?' One wonders how many passers-by really need a laser pointer, but these seem particularly popular at night. Speak to them in Chinese and the Fu Manchu façade evaporates. Suddenly they are people once more, wives and husbands panhandling for the family. It is the capitalist hustle that reduces them to hungry hawkers, while the government wrings its hands and notes that none of these people are supposed to have left their hometowns in the first place.

Arguably, there are also elements of it that are manifest closer to home. Two thousand Tibetans bleed across the Himalayas into Nepal each year. North Koreans sneak to South Korea by moving through the black economy of northeast China, where their presence is hidden among China's 'Korean' minority, unsanctioned by the authorities and invites deportation if they are caught. The grubby man in the Camden street who offers you a pirated DVD, or the anonymous cockle-picker washed ashore at Morecambe Bay – these Chinese are also likely to be at the end of a journey that began with farm lay-offs in some distant interior province. In the cruel slang of London's Chinatown, the more-travelled restaurant employees call them 'dumb waiters', for their inability to speak English.

Their fate, of course, is no different from that of migrant workers throughout history. The difference lies in the sheer size of the migration, and its impact on China itself – an invisible nation, with a population at least four times the size of the United Kingdom, going literally off the books and disappearing into suburban slums, placing unexpected demands on the infrastructures of power, sewage and water, nickel-and-diming at the edges of the black economy, and inflating the statistics for crime and disease.

▶ Hu matters

The first decade of the 21st century saw two disease outbreaks, SARS and H5N1 'bird flu', both traced to China, and believed to stem from poor food hygiene or corner-cutting in remote communities. China's handling of both incidents points to a possible increase of problems for a state that operates on authoritarian, secretive levels in a globalized economy. Meanwhile, odd news items such as the sudden ousting of Bo Xilai, Party chief in Chongqing, point to a continued power struggle among the 'princelings' – the privileged heirs of the old Party elite.

While some Western observers might hope that increased affluence in China will lead to increased accommodation of reform and liberalization, this is not how it appears to the Party. In 2011, Wu Bangguo of the National People's Congress gave a speech outlining 'Five Nos' that should define Party attitudes for the near future: 'No multi-party election; no diversified guiding principles, no separation of powers, no federal system, and no privatization.' In other words, business as usual, but with more BMWs.

Instead of election campaigns and debates, China seems to have flurries of scandal immediately preceding any change in power: Lin Biao, heir apparent in the 1960s, suddenly dead under suspicious circumstances and posthumously accused of plotting a coup; Chen Liangyu, leader of Shanghai in the 2000s, suddenly brought down before the 17th Party Congress; Bo Xilai, suddenly embroiled in a corruption scandal mere months before he was expected to take power at the 18th Party Congress.

It has been suggested that these events were, if not engineered by figures in power, then perhaps 'allowed to happen' through judicious removal of the censor – Bo Xilai, in particular, seemed to become conspicuously fair game for internet attacks shortly before his downfall.

There is, of course, a difference between witch-hunts and due diligence. Chinese industrial successes are edged aside in foreign reporting in favour of horror stories of 'quality fade', corporate swindles and cooked books. China has yet to address issues of transparency and quality control, in part because it often sees international standards as the imposition of a foreign (usually American) hegemony, which in turn evokes memories of the Century of Humiliation.

Where Deng Xiaoping once spoke of the glory of getting rich, many in the ruling elite of China undoubtedly now *are*, along with the teeming millions of China's urban middle class. This brings the Communist Party into confrontation with its origins in revolution, and its slow transformation into an institution of government, but an institution that remains permanently wary of any obvious attempts to change it. As a one-party state, ever promoting its notion of 'harmony', China lacks something that we in the West all too often take for granted. It lacks a loyal opposition.

The very word 'lack', of course, betrays my Western bias. On paper, China is not even a 'one-party state', since several vestigial democratic parties continue to rubber-stamp Communist Party proclamations. Nor is it unchangeable, as demonstrated by the immense changes wrought during the Deng era. But there is no way of effecting change except from within the Party. The Party might present the face of a single, unanimous monolith, but its shadows hide conservatives and liberals, reformers and retrenchers, leftists and rightists. It encompasses the good, the bad and the ugly, and more often than not in foreign reporting, it is only the last two who get the attention.

Some political commentators have called Hu Jintao's period in office a 'lost decade', as he simply coasted on the ideas already put into action by Jiang Zemin, himself often merely perpetuating reforms instituted by Deng Xiaoping. The first decade of the 21st century saw China rise to unbelievable heights. The second decade will be characterized by the question of how it can maintain such achievements, amid mounting challenges in social equality, sustainability and ecology. These factors are sure to characterize the presidency of Xi Jinping, who took office on 14 March 2013.

5

The Chinese future

There are some bored foreigners, with full stomachs, who have nothing better to do than point fingers at us. First, China doesn't export revolution; second, China doesn't export hunger and poverty; third, China doesn't come and cause you headaches. What more is there to be said?

Xi Jinping

As per the foggier resolve and spin control of the 21st century, the 12th 'Five-Year Plan' of the People's Republic of China, covering the years 2011–15, is less of a plan and more of a *guideline*. However, its aims clearly set out the immense difference between the China of Mao's 1949 Tiananmen proclamation and the China of 2015. The proposals for the immediate future included a new airport in Beijing, targets for reaching 83,000 km of highways, and 45,000 km of high-speed rail, and the expectation that, for the first time, more than half of the Chinese population will be living in cities.

There are plans for 36 million affordable apartments, and incentives for new industries, particularly on the urbanized coast. The ghost of Deng Xiaoping would be pleased with guidelines calling for foreign investment in high-tech and green ventures, and in a gentle nudge for China's great coastal megalopolis to drift away from grimy industries towards research, technology and an economy increasingly reliant on services and consumption. Chairman Mao, however, would surely be aghast at a China that continues to drift ever closer towards capitalism, dismantling even more of the collective ownership of the Communist era. All except the ever-present Party, which often has a controlling interest in the new ventures, and the ability to hire and fire executives.

China remains an authoritarian state, able to push through macro-structures and massive projects without quite so much of the red tape (or some might say, safety concerns) of more liberal nations. Sustainability initiatives and ecologically minded developments are

▲ Portraits of China's first four leaders share the limelight at the 60th anniversary celebrations in 2009 (left to right: Mao Zedong, Deng Xiaoping, Jiang Zemin and Hu Jintao).

arguably *easier* to enforce in such a state, although the Plan also calls for increased investment in nuclear power, liable to worry foreign pundits in an age that still remembers Three Mile Island and Chernobyl, not to mention Fukushima.

In a century sure to be characterized by challenges in energy and ecology, China boasts a huge land area, massive reserves of coal and minerals, and the potential might to seize other resources from neighbouring regions, be it Uzbek gas or Siberian lumber. The economist Chi Fulin, in *The Road to China's Prosperity*, outlines areas for reform and development between now and the year 2029, highlighting the continued move from production to consumption and emphasizing the continued growth of an affluent middle class, projected to reach 600 million by 2025. But although he cannot (indeed dare not) offer any pathways outside the Party line, he does recognize the need for 'safety valves' that will allow Chinese citizens to effect change at a local level – consultations, referenda on local issues and arbitration schemes. For the Party itself, he advises the maintenance of a firm, fair tax and finance system, so that the same middle class does not feel that its new wealth is at risk.

▶ Energy and resources

China's economic might has been a popular topic since long before Western businessmen began enthusing about the possibility of 'a billion cans of cola' every day. Today, the expansion and consolidation of Chinese industry, coupled with competitive rates and a sweatshop labour force, has awarded China a huge share of certain world markets. There are factories in south China that produce most of the world's denim jeans. As Jonathan Fenby notes in the *Penguin History of Modern China*, Zhejiang province alone produces 'a third of the world's socks, 40 per cent of its ties, and 70 per cent of its cigarette lighters, as well as 350 million umbrellas a year and a billion decks of playing cards.'

We feel the impact of China's economy in other ways, not merely in the price of shoes. China's meteoric progress requires raw materials, many of which have to be sourced from elsewhere. Half the world's construction cranes are in China, where some wags have christened them the new national bird. These metal giants loom over construction sites that consume large quantities of the world's concrete, and inflate scrap metal prices thousands of miles away. When a London train is delayed because someone has stolen power or communications cables, or when a street is jammed because a manhole cover has gone missing, this is an odd but palpable way that China matters even to people who never give it any thought.

In a footnote to Marx's *Das Kapital*, Friedrich Engels predicted the ultimate cost of the integration of Chinese labour into a global economy – everything would be dragged down to the level of 'Chinese wages'. While Western commentators may shake their heads at China's poor working conditions, lax safety standards and flouting of intellectual property law, we must also face the daunting prospect that China is not a developing country striving towards a Western 'norm'. Instead, could it be a glimpse of where we are all headed, a future of declining standards of living, runaway climate change and climbing population pressures? It matters to all of us that we have cheap shoes and ready access to umbrellas. Capitalism is a worldwide pyramid scheme, but what happens when there is nowhere left to manufacture cheaply? Sustainability is not merely a matter of resources, but of services – Chi Fulin believes that green technology offers the best chance of China creating jobs and wealth without using resources. Already, the high-speed rail network is creating new jobs while reducing carbon footprints. Chi foresees further large-scale projects for power generation and environmental clean-up that will create greener prosperity.

▶ Gender and demographics

Women's issues were an important part of revolutionary thought, with early reformers seeking to remove patriarchy and chauvinism. 'Women hold up half the sky', noted a young Chairman Mao, who uncompromisingly compared arranged marriages to 'rape' of a child by its parents. The most prominent act of reform in the 20th century was the rescue of Chinese women from foot-binding, a ghastly tradition that left many Chinese women crippled. One of the first acts of the newly founded People's Republic was the promulgation of a new Marriage Law, designed to break with thousands of years of tradition. Marriage was to be a decision entered into by two people, without pressure from their families, and it was to be a simple decision taken for reasons of companionship and increased productivity. People should get married because they were happier workers together – the new law refused to acknowledge any difference between legitimate and illegitimate children, and many modern Chinese wives kept their maiden name.

In practice, neither the original Marriage Law nor its revision in 1980 have removed all elements of the past, and it would be naïve to expect them to. Chinese weddings remain lavish and materialist affairs, loaded with both ancient traditions and borrowings from Western ceremonies – they are likely to remain so, because the industry servicing the demand is precisely the sort of consumption on which post-modern economies rely.

The 'one-child' policy has been controversial for several reasons. At its 'soft' end, it amounts to little more than inspirational posters and voluntary birth control. But it has been associated with invasive scrutiny of people's private lives, including what amounts to a neighbourhood watch of who is menstruating. There is also the inevitable, unpleasant question of how the policy should be enforced in the event of an infringement. The media, both inside and outside China, became particularly animated in 2012 when Feng Jianmei, a woman who could not afford to pay the fine for a second child, was forced to have an abortion at seven months, and later photographed with her dead foetus at her bedside.

In an inadvertent irony, the scandal broke at the time the official press were trumpeting women's rights, in the build-up to the launch of China's first female astronaut.

Ever since the implementation of the one-child policy, there have also been echoes of even more sinister issues. Despite government advertising extolling the virtues of daughters and arguing, somewhat defensively, that girls were just as good as boys, the Chinese population since the 1980s has shown a marked bias towards male births. There have been accusations of female infanticide and abortions steered by gender. But there is also the potential problem of the 'Army of Bachelors' – 37 million Chinese men who will never find a bride in their own generation, another potential crucible of discontent.

The one-child policy has created a tipping point in gender relations, flooding universities, for example, with go-getting daughters whose only-child status garners them a familial support that might have otherwise been conferred upon a brother. The Chinese media has been swift to characterize this new generation as fickle and pushy, with women, in the minority, able to pick and choose deftly among potential suitors, and to place heavy materialist demands on any ideal husband.

Romance might not be dead in China, but it is certainly expensive. Among a generation of women demanding minimum height, qualifications and salaries among suitors, the fashion model Ma Nuo became something of an icon of modern, materialist girl power when she said: 'I would rather cry in the back of a BMW than laugh on the back of a bicycle.'

The Chinese future

▲ Chinese women arguably have the upper hand when it comes to picking a potential husband.

One of the sights liable to prove most surprising to today's visitor to China is the vast number of shopping malls, loaded with foreign brands but seemingly lacking customers. You wander polished marble floors stocked with L'Oreal and Mulberry, and wonder where the customers are. Colossal investment in such designer outlets is another leap of faith on the part of investors. The marketing analyst Mary Bergstrom cites data that points to the immense potential of the Chinese middle class, starting with the many aspirational purchases of *nouveaux* arrivals who want to signify their rise to the top with a Louis Vuitton bag or a squirt of Chanel Nº 5. But she also notes the surprising conclusion of a survey in 2008, that up to a third of the Chinese luxury goods market comprises trinkets and baubles purchased by rich men for their mistresses – far from being wiped out by modernity, old-fashioned concubinage could be said to be driving China's capitalist economy.

China also faces the same problem as other developed societies – a 'greying' population that will gradually outnumber the young. Exacerbated by the one-child policy, China faces the prospect that 35 per cent of the population will be over 50 by 2025, and 42 per cent by 2050. This will play havoc with pension schemes, particularly when the traditional safety net, of parents living with their son's family, will be unlikely for those whose only daughters have married and moved away.

Race, too, is a demographic issue for the Party. The Han Chinese ethnic majority represents 90 per cent of the population of China, and is what is most usually meant when people refer to 'the Chinese'. But what of the other 100 million citizens? An argument has begun within the Party to abolish all ethnicities, removing the part of national ID cards that specifies whether someone is Han or Manchu or Uyghur or Tibetan. While this certainly fulfils Communist ideals of one nation, one party and one people, it will surely not remove inequalities and tensions.

The ethnic minorities are largely clustered in the west of China, away from the prosperous coast. Throughout the history of modern China, Chinese history and culture has usually meant Han history and culture. Uyghurs must attend schools taught in Mandarin, distancing them from their cousins across the border in the various Central Asian 'Stans. Tibetans are now connected to Beijing by a direct rail link, which brings in increasing numbers of Han colonists. The lifestyle of the nomadic Inner Mongolians has become increasingly sedentary, threatening in turn many traditional aspects of their culture. Such issues plague minorities all over the world, but there are almost as many ethnic minority citizens in China as there are Japanese in Japan. They form an important, albeit often invisible, bloc within China, a site of economic disadvantage, unseen diversity and potential unrest.

▶ Airpocalypse

China's great leap in the last 20 years has exerted an environmental cost. Since 2007, China has emitted more greenhouse gases than the USA. On average, China opens a new coal-fired power station every week. Beijing has always been plagued by sandstorms out of the Gobi Desert, and it is customary for residents in a town to begin to assume that limited visibility is normal. Nobody who has experienced a murky Beijing dust storm can deny that the desert is close at hand. But it is getting closer, and growing at a rate of 2,000 square miles a year. Sand and smog have contributed to a decline in air quality so visible that you can literally see it hanging in the air within some large indoor spaces such as railway stations.

▲ Face masks are now a common sight in Beijing's streets, as locals attempt to live with the poor air quality.

The US embassy in Beijing has recorded impurities in the air using a stricter scale than the Party for its measurements, and testing for smaller and arguably more dangerous particles, more likely to lodge in the lungs. If the pollution monitoring index has a rating over 150, it is regarded as 'harmful' for anyone who suffers long-term exposure. Above 300, it is 'hazardous'. In January 2013, the embassy posted a score of 755, suggesting that the Beijing air was truly toxic. The Chinese media was sluggish to react, at first berating the Americans for interfering in a local matter, and then questioning their statistics. For a brief period around Chinese New Year, they even blamed excessive fireworks for the citywide smog. But when it proved to be more than a New Year one-off, reporting began to engage with it, noting that many Beijingers wore masks, that visibility had been known to diminish to little more than 50 feet, that the air was indeed unhealthy and that doing something about pollution was already a policy in the new Five-Year Plan.

What such reporting fails to note is that similar pollution issues affect *every* major Chinese city. Coal power and heavy industry are ubiquitous, and Beijing is merely the city lucky enough to have interfering American ambassadorial staff, determined to investigate why they can't stop coughing. In Luoyang, it is no longer possible to see the other side of the street. Even tourist cities like Xi'an are often wreathed in dense fog. Chinese environmentalists point to the infamous London smog of 1952, not only as a precedent, but also as a sign of hope, that things can and should improve.

▶ Chinas at home and abroad

There remains a strong disparity in income between the Chinese mega-cities and the outlying provinces. There are multiple 'Chinas', many of them equivalent in size to an entire European nation, although of course some of the populations overlap. There is the China of middle-class yuppies, with a current population of some 150 million – the market for Tissot watches and L'Occitane shower gel. There are the adult Chinese considered to be illiterate: 110 million. There is the China of dispossessed migrants, 150 million people, scrabbling to make a living in slums and sweatshops. There is the China of people still living in abject poverty. 76 million There is the China of non-Han ethnic minorities – the 120 million Manchus, Muslims, Tibetans Hakka and others. There is the China beyond the People's Republic, of nearly 3 million in Singapore and 23 million on Taiwan.

Then there are the overseas Chinese who form significant enclaves within other countries, enriching their economies and cultures for centuries, often in the face of racial prejudice – 5 million in North America; a million in Russia, another million in Vietnam and 800,000 in Australia. Fifteen million split between Indonesia and Malaysia. There are half a million Chinese in Great Britain and 400,000 in Venezuela. Many of these people are fully assimilated into their new homelands, which often leaves them disregarded in any discussion of 'China and the Chinese'. But while they may carry foreign passports and pledge allegiance to other flags (a source of deep suspicion before the pragmatic reforms of Deng Xiaoping), they form an important cultural and economic bloc – sources of investment and tourism, or ready markets for specifically Chinese goods.

In Indonesia, Cambodia and Myanmar, they can be harder to spot, since until recently it was illegal to be a local citizen with a foreign name. Similarly, in Thailand, local regulations require residents to have a Thai name to own property, but there are 10 million Thais of Chinese descent. An estimated three-quarters of a million residents of Africa are Chinese citizens on long-term employment contracts. The character of such overseas communities is a fascinating patchwork of Chinese linguistics – Britain's Chinatowns ring with the Cantonese dialect, reflecting connections to Hong Kong and the south. A third of New York's Chinese speak variants of Hokkien, the language of the south-western province of Fujian and of Taiwan across the water. In Thailand and Indonesia, family conversations and the spelling of names are more likely to reflect Teochew, the dialect spoken around Chaozhou in Guangdong province.

Although miscegenation, 'passing' as local and simple head-counts are inexact, the global population of Chinese outside China, both by descent and as expatriate labourers, is estimated at something around 120 million. They are a substantial part of the Chinese market, both as investors and as consumers.

Jonathan Fenby, in the *Penguin History of Modern China*, goes so far as to call China 'the last great colonial empire on earth', alluding to its possessions in Tibet and Xinjiang. You will not hear such words from Chinese citizens, who have been taught that both territories have 'always' been part of China – and certainly both of them have a longer history as part of China than the United States of America has as a nation. But colonial echoes are not merely a matter of conquered territories, but also of overseas outposts serving an affluent centre. China's labour force forms a cornerstone of overseas markets, dominating everything from street hawker pitches in Russia to the discount supermarket sector in Argentina.

China Development Bank, wholly owned by the Party and financed through bonds, is a powerful organ of China's state capitalism. Although not overtly part of China's foreign policy, it is a larger overseas entity than the World Bank, and has invested immense amounts of Chinese capital in Third World infrastructure projects, from African railways to a gas pipeline in Turkmenistan. It has already invested to the tune of US$40 billion in the oil-rich Venezuelan economy, making China a new player in the volatile Central American region. It is similarly involved in development loans that bolster Ethiopian manufacturing and Ghanaian mining. China's involvement in the global economy is hence far more direct and intimate than may at first be apparent. No longer self-sufficient in oil, China is establishing lines of supply abroad, sure to bring it ultimately into competition with other nations. None of this is anything new in the history of colonialism and globalization, and many of the achievements and opportunities mirror those that existed for European investors in China in the 19th century. It is a far cry from the insular, socialist initiatives of the Mao era, but it remains a clutch of international issues sure to attract the attention of China's leadership in the 21st century.

▶ All that matters?

Media opinion of China's prospects often seems divided between world-beating triumphalism and horrific doomsday scenarios. China remains a major manufacturing power, and a military force now developing beyond its traditional units to submarines and an aircraft carrier. Where once Chinese hawks fretted about the 'threat' from Taiwan, they now counsel a Chinese military force that is ready to spring to the aid of Chinese citizens in far-flung corners of the globe.

Modern China has become a leading lender to foreign powers, a player in American stocks, and a major investor in African economies. The Party continues to maintain strict controls on information against the threat of new information sources, leading to the Great Firewall of China that limits internet access. Discussion of China's history is still censored in China itself, strongly favouring Party-approved narratives.

Meanwhile, certain elements within the Party itself suggest a new elite that simply buys its way to privilege, blithely paying the fines for having extra children, and then sending those children abroad to benefit from a foreign education. The one-child policy has created a double demographic time-bomb. The favouring of male offspring over female has created an 'Army of Bachelors' unlikely to ever find a wife. The last time China had such an imbalance of men was just before the Taiping Rebellion.

In the months before he rose to the rank of Premier in 2012, Li Keqiang recommended that the cadres in his circle (and anyone with an interest in policy) read Alexis de Tocqueville's *Ancien Regime and the French Revolution*. It is a fascinating choice for a Chinese leader, and suitably foreign in its subject matter to avoid ruffling any local feathers. There is not a word, of course, in Ancien Regime about Chairman Mao, but it has much to say about the misdeeds of Napoleon. There is much about the principles on which a revolution is founded, and praise for the eternal quest to achieve goals of equality and, yes, liberty.

Throughout the writing of this book, I have asked myself what *truly* matters. Not the historical issues soon to be papered over by China's traditionally amnesiac historiography; not boundary disputes and sovereignty sure to fade as populations merge and living standards balance. Both Communist China and Western liberal democracy regard themselves as the 'end of history' – a final organizational step across the finish line towards a system that, while never perfect, can strive to make itself ever better. But in China, there is no opposition party carping about the failures of the ruling regime. Any change or reform must come from within, in an environment hostile to overt criticism, and in a mood that constantly asserts that all is well. There are, undoubtedly, factions within the Communist Party that dispute over issues of policy, but their aims and powers are hard to see. Dissenting voices are studiously ignored or made to disappear. To be part of the conversation, any Chinese thinker must already concede an accommodation with Party power, or be dismissed as a dissident.

Mao spoke of 475 million Chinese people standing up. There are now three times as many in a nation perhaps more deserving than ever before of its name, Zhong Guo, or the 'Middle Kingdom'. In a world of changing climates, limited resources and runaway pollution, decisions made in Modern China have the pivotal power to steer the fate of the whole world for good or ill. In all sorts of ways, including purchasing power, competition, consumption and investment, the Chinese will have a significant say in how bright our future can be – and that matters to us all.

Seven leaders of the Chinese Communist Party

1 **Chairman Mao Zedong** (1945–76). An early member of the Chinese Communist Party, Mao somehow survived 20 years of in-fighting, guerrilla warfare and reversals of fortune to become Party Chairman in 1945. Officially sharing power with the Premier Zhou Enlai, he deftly held onto his position by manipulating his role as the interpreter of Communist doctrine, initiating deluded schemes that would ultimately cause the deaths of millions.

2 **Chairman Hua Guofeng** (1976–81). A loyal protégé of Mao, Hua took over from Zhou Enlai as Premier, and was able to outmanoeuvre the 'Gang of Four', led by Mao's wife, who hoped to succeed the Chairman on his death. He was ousted in 1978 by Deng Xiaoping, but stayed in power for two more years, and remained a politician until 2002. The announcement of his death was swamped by coverage of the ongoing Beijing Olympics.

3 **Chairman Hu Yaobang** (1981–7). One of the first high-profile figures to abandon the anonymous 'Mao suit', Hu was also quick to abandon Mao, controversially stating that none of the late Chairman's theories

were worth preserving. A reformer who initiated many changes on behalf of Deng Xiaoping, Hu was also famed for his desire for reconciliation with Japan, and for his willingness to embrace foreign ideas – he even once notoriously suggested that the Chinese avoid communicable diseases by eating individual portions with knives and forks. His death in 1989 was the initial excuse for the assembly of 'mourners' in Tiananmen Square, leading to the famous protests.

4   **General Secretary Zhao Ziyang** (1987–9). Instrumental in Mao's Great Leap Forward, Zhao was purged during the Cultural Revolution, only to be swept back into power in the early 1970s. His controversial market-oriented reforms in Sichuan were an inspiration to Deng Xiaoping, and he presided over the period in which the Chinese press was arguably at its most free. During a souring relationship with Deng, his public attempt to reason with the Tiananmen protesters would be his downfall, and it led to 15 years under house arrest. *Prisoner of the State*, his memoir, was smuggled out on cassette tapes and eventually published.

5   **General Secretary Jiang Zemin** (1989–2002). Born in 1926 and adopted by his widowed aunt after the death of his war hero father. Graduated in electrical engineering and learned on the job at the Stalin Automobile Works, Moscow. Transferred to government service after a career in vehicle manufacture, as the Minister for Electronic

Industries in 1983. Famous for his command of foreign languages, and for once reciting the Gettysburg Address, in English, to quell a student demonstration. Noted for the 'Three Represents' theory, claiming that the Party represents the will of the people in Revolution, Construction [of the nation] and Reform.

6 **General Secretary Hu Jintao** (2002–12). Born in 1942, the son of a tea trader and a teacher. Chairman of Tsinghua University student union, and a graduate in hydraulic engineering. Worked in hydroelectric power until 1973, when he swiftly rose through the Party ranks during a scheme to promote revolutionaries and specialists. Shuffled to Tibet, where he imposed martial law in 1989. Promoted 'Eight Honours and Disgraces' setting out how Party members should behave, but is more likely to be remembered for his pronouncements on the need for a 'harmonious' society.

7 **General Secretary Xi Jinping** (2012–). A fast riser in the Party, Xi is the son of Xi Zhongxun, a former wartime guerrilla and Vice-Premier – making him one of the 'princelings' who form the young Party in-crowd. Xi's career has been distinguished by an absence of political scandals in any of his provincial postings. A chemical engineer married to a celebrity singer in the People's Liberation Army, he has been instrumental in many high-profile projects in recent years, including the preparations for the Beijing Olympics and Hong Kong/Macau handovers.

'Two Whatevers'

Chairman Hua Guofeng (1976–81) founded his office on the guiding principles of his 'Two Whatevers', which would have been a safe tactic only a couple of years before, but soon led to his dismissal in the reform minded 1980s:

8 To follow whatever policy Mao had decreed.

9 To stick to whatever instructions Mao had given.

Ten Chinese city slogans

With so much tradition bulldozed and razed, it can often be difficult telling Chinese cities apart – a particular issue when one is seeking to invest, build factories or otherwise commit finances to a long-term project in any one location. Many Chinese cities have attempted to brand themselves with some definable quality that separates one anonymous collection of skyscrapers from other, although sometimes even this branding can achieve a certain homogeneity – at least seven different Chinese cities have attempted to persuade visitors that they are 'the Oriental Geneva'.

10 **Beijing**: 'Beijing Spirit', which, upon further enquiry, turns out to comprise: 'Patriotism, Innovation, Inclusiveness and Virtue'. The words were picked from a citywide vote, although 'only' a couple of million Beijingers participated.

11 **Chengdu**: 'Capital of Success, Capital of Colour, Capital of Cuisine'.

12 **Chongqing**: 'If You've Never Been to Chongqing, You Don't Know China.'

13 **Hangzhou**: 'Exquisite and Harmonious, Magnanimous and Open-Minded'.

14 **Hong Kong**: 'Asia's World City'.

15 **Kunming**: 'Every Day is Spring.'

16 **Ningbo**: 'Honest, Pragmatic, Open-Minded, Innovative'.

17 **Rizhao**: 'Blue Skies, Turquoise Seas, Golden Beaches'.

18 **Shanghai**: 'Wonderful Every Day'.

19 **Yichun**: 'A City Called Spring'. This slogan, introduced in 2010, did not last long; it transpired that it was a double-entendre and also meant 'The City of Orgasmic Gasps'.

Ten books on modern China

20 *Factory Girls: Voices from the Heart of Modern China*. Leslie T. Chang lives among the migrant workers of south China, tracing the life stories of several women with varying degrees of success. An illuminating glimpse of many of the issues affecting China's working class.

21 *The Last Days of Old Beijing: Life in the Vanishing Backstreets of a City Transformed*. Michael Meyer witnesses the revolutionary transformation of China's capital as the 2008 Olympics approaches

and huge areas of the old city are bulldozed. A fine testament to the lives of everyday locals – similarly made over, whether they wanted it or not.

22 *Deng Xiaoping and the Transformation of Modern China*. Ezra Vogel's mammoth biography explains how a quiet, unassuming man somehow became the catalyst for China's emergence from its Mao-era cocoon. Mao's face is still all over the media, but it's Deng who truly matters in understanding the changes of the last 30 years.

23 *All Eyes East: Lessons from the Front Lines of Marketing to China's Youth*. Mary Bergstrom's account is rooted firmly in hard data, and offers many surprising and eye-popping conclusions about the present condition and likely future directions of the Chinese market.

24 *The Twelfth Five-Year Plan for National Economic and Social Development of the People's Republic of China*. Running to 293 pages in the English translation, this is the statement of all that matters to the Communist Party, including projected figures and policy ideas. The Plan is notable sometimes more for what isn't mentioned than what is. There is significantly more discussion of the value of sport than of art and literature, for example. Some aspirations are clearly rather hopeful – not much immediate chance of the projected rail link to Taipei, one imagines.

25 *The Chinese Dream: The Rise of the World's Largest Middle Class and What it Means to You*. Helen Wang discusses the aspirations and beliefs of the people who are supposed to be buying all those Nike trainers and iPhones.

26 *Ancien Regime and the French Revolution*. Alexis de Tocqueville's 1864 treatise has become mandatory reading for all China-watchers since it was revealed that the new premier Li Keqiang had recommended it to his colleagues. With its discussion of the role and origins of revolution, the abandonment of the countryside, and how prosperity and reform themselves can cause unrest, it offers much food for thought.

27 *The Road to China's Prosperity in the Next Three Decades*. Chi Fulin, the chairman of the research committee advising on the Twelfth Five-Year Plan, looks ahead even further, to 2039. Along with his other book, *Consumption-led Growth* it amounts to a blueprint of current trends in Party thinking, and offers a few clues as to the *next* Five-Year Plan, ascribing particular importance to China's forthcoming role in a global 'low-carbon economy'.

28 *China 3.0*. Editor Mark Leonard, from the European Council on Foreign Relations, suggests that a new era is beginning, after 30 years of Mao's influence and another 30 of Deng's. But what can we expect in the next three decades? Leonard rounds up thinkers from China's New Left and New Right, Neo-Conservatives and Neo-Maoists, and gives each of them a soapbox.

29 *China Dreams: 20 Visions of the Future*, by William A. Callahan, poses similar questions to 'citizen-intellectuals', for a series of arguments for things to come, expressed in terms of business forecasts, ethnic discourses and the continuing influence of powerful local hubs such as Shanghai and Chongqing.

Nine search terms blocked on the Chinese internet

30 Communist bandits (old Nationalist propaganda term)

31 Dalai [Lama] (Spiritual leader of Tibet)

32 Re-education through Labour (Cultural Revolution phrase)

33 Democratic Progressive Party (Taiwan's pro-independence party)

34 4 June (date of the Tiananmen Square incident)

35 Tank Man (Tiananmen Square icon)

36 Falun Gong (banned religious cult)

37 Voice of America (US broadcaster)

38 Huahua Gongzi (Chinese name of *Playboy* magazine)

Seven great China travel books

39 *Behind the Great Wall*, by Colin Thubron, is arguably the greatest modern Chinese travel book, and preserves a snapshot of life during the incredible transformations of the Deng Xiaoping era.

40 *Red Dust: A Path through China*, by Ma Jian, is a 1980s journey from Beijing to Tibet and back to the coast, looping in and over itself through much of China. He visits many of the same places as Thubron, but with the anonymity and access afforded to a Chinese citizen.

41 *The River at the Centre of the World: A Journey up the Yangtze, and Back in Chinese Time*, by Simon Winchester, does exactly what it says on the tin, and is a delightful account of China in the 1990s.

42 *Country Driving: A Chinese Road Trip*, by Peter Hessler, begins as an attempt to travel along the Great Wall by car, but morphs into an account of his DIY exploits in a village outside Beijing.

43 *China Road: A Journey into the Future of a Rising Power*, by Rob Gifford, follows the highway that leads east–west from Shanghai to Kazakhstan, offering valuable insights on modern China, warts and all.

44 *The Horse that Leaps through Clouds: A Tale of Espionage, the Silk Road and the Rise of Modern China*, by Eric Enno Tamm, is a journey from west to east across China from Kashgar to Beijing, in the footsteps of the 1906 explorer Gustaf Mannerheim, assessing the impact of a century of troubles.

45 *Invisible China: A Journey through Ethnic Borderlands*, by Colin Legerton and Jacob Rawson, charts 14,000 kilometres of travel by bus and train, through many of China's minority communities.

Ten ethnic 'minorities' in China

46 Zhuang (Guangxi natives): 16.9 million

47 Hui (Muslims): 10.6 million

48 Manchu: 10.4 million

49 Uyghurs (Xinjiang): 10.1 million

50 Tibetans: 6.3 million

51 Mongols: 6 million

52 Koreans: 1.8 million

53 Kazakh: 1.5 million

54 Russians: 15,393

55 Naturalized immigrants: 1,445

Ten great China websites

56 *Danwei* is a blog that translates and aggregates breaking news stories from China.

www.danwei.com

57 *The Marco Polo Project* uploads fiction and non-fiction from emerging Chinese writers, with an ongoing translation policy that makes as much as possible available in both English and Chinese.

http://marcopoloproject.org

58 *The Sinica Podcasts*, presented by Kaiser Kuo and Danwei's Jeremy Goldkorn, present a regular insight into the heart of current affairs in China. Witty and informed, it also features many heavy-hitting guests from the world of China journalism. Hosted by *Pop-Up Chinese*, itself a handy site for language-learning.

http://popupchinese.com/feeds/custom/sinica

59 *Beijing Cream*, 'a dollop of China', snuffles like a truffle pig for gems of Chinese reportage and gossip. A great place to find whatever oddness is trending at this very moment, from newspaper scandals to internet memes.

http://beijingcream.com

60 *The Shanghaiist*. Not to be outdone, Shanghai bloggers offer scrapings from web adverts, newspapers and corporate malpractice reports.

http://shanghaiist.com

61 *Far West China*. A blog dedicated to life and news in Xinjiang, which takes up a sixth of China's landmass and has most of the oil – and much of the controversy.

www.farwestchina.com

62 *China Law Blog*. Detailed insights and commentary on Chinese law and business, negotiating the thorny pathways of getting stuff done.

www.chinalawblog.com

63 *The China Story* is a project by the Australian National University to chronicle key issues in contemporary China. As the name implies, it concentrates on narratives from different perspectives, contrasting government decrees with grass-roots reportage, dissident protest and foreign punditry, and often suggesting that the truth belongs to none of the above. Don't miss their free Yearbook – packed with insight.

www.thechinastory.org

64 Tea Leaf Nation aspires to be the website that China experts read, and meets this goal with numerous insightful articles on emerging issues – including the international network of powdered milk sales to Chinese mothers, schools for hackers and expat life.

www.tealeafnation.com

65 *Marketing to China* collates new research, useful statistics and illuminating anecdotes about business in the People's Republic. An interesting snapshot of new trends, import/export opportunities and cautionary tales.

http://marketingtochina.com

Ten websites you can't see from China

66 Google Docs

67 WordPress

68 Facebook

69 Twitter

70 YouTube

71 Internet Movie Database

Nine books you won't find in modern China

Books 'banned' in China aren't necessarily slapped down by official government fiat; the Party is well aware that such an act only generates further publicity. Instead, they are more likely to be edged out of listings and warehouses by jumpy lower-level officials who would rather err on the side of caution when it comes to controversial subjects. The result is the same, however – many issues in modern Chinese society are more transparently discussed abroad than at home.

76 *Poorly Made in China: An Insider's Account of the China Production Game*. Paul Midler's semi-autobiographical confessions lift the lid on corner-cutting, 'quality fade' and double-crossing in the factories of south China. Depending on where one stands, either a searing indictment of Chinese business culture or an account of how swiftly and precisely the Chinese have adopted the principles of globalized capitalism.

77 *The End of Cheap China: Economic and Cultural Trends That Will Disrupt the World*, by Shaun Rein, remains critical of China's record on food safety, accountability and education, but suggests that the American media creates a China 'threat' which doesn't necessarily exist.

78 *The Rise and Fall of the House of Bo: How a Murder Exposed the Cracks in China's Leadership.* John Garnaut picks over the Bo Xilai scandal, noting the signs of struggles among the 'princelings' and old enmities dating back to the Revolution itself.

79 *The Party: The Secret World of China's Communist Rulers.* Richard McGregor investigates the immense influence of the Communist Party within China's 'state capitalist' system. Although framed as an exposé, it does invite the question: doesn't *every* country have a secretive elite of power brokers, and isn't China's simply easier to spot?

80 *Tombstone: The Untold Story of Mao's Great Famine.* Yang Jisheng is not the first author to write about the Great Leap Forward of 1958–62, but his chilling chronicle of starvation, murder and cannibalism was banned in China, seemingly for presenting evidence that Mao and the party system were culpable in the deaths of millions.

81 *The Fat Years.* Chan Koonchung's 'novel' smuggles in long polemics about the state of modern China, the complacency of its yuppies and the impossibility of effecting change in a one-party state.

82 *China's Silent Army: The Pioneers, Traders, Fixers and Workers Who Are Remaking the World in Beijing's Image.* Juan Pablo Cardenal and Heriberto Araujo report from all around the globe on the way that China is already reaching deeply into our lives. From sweatshops to investment banks, copper mines to shipping containers, they reveal that China already matters to a great degree.

83 *Mr China*. Tim Clissold's book is a business classic and remains a grim, yet still humorous, warning about the slippery nature of Chinese contracts and the pitfalls of foreign investment in the Middle Kingdom.

84 *China's Superbank: Debt, Oil, and Influence – How China Development Bank is Rewriting the Rules of Finance*, by Henry Sanderson and Michael Forsythe, observes that the CDB is actually bigger and more powerful than the World Bank, and lends billions to third-world initiatives.

Five unexpectedly popular foreign TV shows

Even if not legally broadcast, many foreign TV shows are available to Chinese on download or pirate DVD. Their popularity, particularly with the young middle class learning English, has made many of them unexpected ambassadors for soft power.

85 *The Big Bang Theory*. Huge with students who have to sleep four to a room in dorms.

86 *Downton Abbey*. The oddities of the British aristocracy, entertaining the People's Republic.

87 *Sex and the City*. Known as *Hope City* in China.

88 *Friends*. Known as *Old Friends*, or *Six Together*.

89 *Game of Thrones*. Power, politics, dragons...

Three completely different 'modern Chinas'

90 *Singapore*. An island city-state surrounded by Malaysian territory, Singapore's authoritarian but business-driven society was a strong model for Deng Xiaoping, and often cited in his speeches. With a population of 5 million people, it has four official languages, including Mandarin Chinese, spoken by 74 per cent of its citizens.

91 *Taiwan*. The last bastion of the old Republic of China, modern Taiwan is often indistinguishable, at least superficially, from the similarly bustling contemporary cities of the nearby Mainland coast. Martial law was lifted in 1987, and the ruling Nationalist party democratically ceded the government to its opposition from 2000 to 2008.

92 *Hong Kong*. Legally a Special Administrative Region of the People's Republic, Hong Kong is guaranteed this status until 2047. It retains its own currency, and still uses long-form characters. Although Mandarin Chinese and English are the official languages, Cantonese (a 'dialect' as different from Mandarin as English is from Dutch) is most often used. But in July 2012, Hong Kong's new Chief Executive,

C. Y. Leung, made his inaugural speech in Mandarin instead of Hong Kong's Cantonese dialect – a sign of further changes to come?

Eight honours and shames

Hu Jintao's contribution to modern Chinese philosophy took the form of eight steps, not mentioning the Party at all:

93 Love the country; do it no harm.

94 Serve the people; never betray them.

95 Follow science; discard ignorance.

96 Be diligent; not indolent.

97 Be united, help each other; make no gains at others' expense.

98 Be honest and trustworthy; do not sacrifice ethics for profit.

99 Be disciplined and law-abiding; not chaotic and lawless.

100 Live plainly, work hard; do not wallow in luxuries and pleasures.

Index

Acknowledgements

Thanks to Andrew Deacon for reading and commenting on an early draft.

Image Credits